Renegade

Yale UNIVERSITY PRESS

NEW HAVEN & LONDON

Renegade

Henry Miller
and the Making of
Tropic of Cancer

Frederick Turner

Set in Janson type by Integrated Publishing Solutions.
Printed in the United States of America.

Library of Congress Cataloging-in-Publication Data
Turner, Frederick W., 1937–
Renegade : Henry Miller and the making of *Tropic of Cancer* /
Frederick Turner.
    p.   cm. — (Icons of America)
Includes bibliographical references and index.
ISBN 978-0-300-14949-4 (hardback)
    1. Miller, Henry, 1891–1980.—Criticism and interpretation.
2. Miller, Henry, 1891–1980. Tropic of cancer. 3. Politics and
literature—United States—History—20th century. 4. Authors
and publishers—United States—History—20th century.
5. Publishers and publishing—United States—History—20th
century. 6. Censorship—United States—History—20th
century. I. Title.
    PS3525.I5454Z8557   2012
    813'.52—dc22   2011019531

A catalogue record for this book is available from the British Library.

This paper meets the requirements of ANSI/NISO Z39.48-1992
(Permanence of Paper).

10 9 8 7 6 5 4 3 2

ICONS OF AMERICA

Icons of America is a series of short works written by leading scholars, critics, and writers, each of whom tells a new and innovative story about American history and culture through the lens of a single iconic individual, event, object, or cultural phenomenon.

For
Jim Harrison

Contents

Contents

Contents

Part One

"Fuck Everything!"

At the end of August 1931, Henry Miller posted a letter from Paris to his Brooklyn boyhood pal, Emil Schnellock. He wrote as if he were some explorer, poised to plunge alone and unarmed into a wilderness. "I start tomorrow on the Paris book: First person, uncensored, formless— fuck everything!" he exclaimed.

As a telegraphic précis of what would three years later become *Tropic of Cancer*, the concluding six words of this brag are an astonishingly accurate prediction of the book Miller had somehow discovered he must write. When it was published in Paris in September 1934 by a man who dealt in what today would be called "soft pornography," it completely fulfilled the bravado of Miller's proclamation, especially in its sustained tone of savage abandon—"fuck everything!"

The expression is, of course, street-corner argot for the defiant impulse to hurl aside all considerations, conventions, and costs and to strike out recklessly into uncharted territory and there achieve personally unprecedented success—or a final failure. Defiant though it is, the impulse must ultimately come from a profound sense of failure, of having been balked and defeated at every turn so that at last there is nothing left to lose. The successful don't have to say, "Fuck everything!" Failures might, and in that deadness of late August in Depression-era Paris Henry Miller definitely belonged in the latter category: he'd apparently lost everything, nationality, job, wife, even his language, which he couldn't use in this foreign place.

On a more literal plane, the book Miller was about to embark on was one in which the narrator and his lawless companions do indeed try to "fuck everything," even perhaps so unlikely a target as the one-legged hooker Miller mentions in telling detail as he used to pass her nightly stand in the Place de Clichy:

> After midnight she stands there in her black rig
> rooted to the spot. Back of her is the little alleyway
> that blazes like an inferno. Passing her now with a
> light heart she reminds me somehow of a goose tied

to a stake, a goose with a diseased liver, so that the world may have its *paté de fois gras*. Must be strange taking that wooden stump to bed with you. One imagines all sorts of things—splinters, etc. However, each man to his taste.

It was passages like this in which a profoundly forbidden form of sex is described with a cruel humor that prompted American tourists in Paris to smuggle home copies of the banned book soon after Jack Kahane's Obelisk Press published it. They kept on doing so until the war interrupted travel to the continent. At the war's end GIs discovered the book, and then eventually the tourists returned to guiltily and gleefully carry it back to the States wrapped in shirts or shawls. By the 1950s *Tropic of Cancer* had acquired a folkloric status while its author wore with an increasing unease the shadowy reputation as a writer of truly "dirty books"—or, as he occasionally styled himself with some bitterness, a "gangster author."

Something of this reputation clings to Miller still, like smoke, though he is long dead. And yet over the years since 1934, and particularly since Barney Rosset's Grove Press triumphed over the censors and published an American edition of *Cancer* in 1961, a simultaneous process has been at work. In it Miller's purely literary reputation has steadily risen so that now he is generally—if somewhat grudgingly—acknowledged to be a major American writer, maybe even a great one. And *Tropic of Cancer*, his first published novel, has risen from smuggled dirty book to American classic, a work that belongs on a select shelf of works that best tell us who we are, for better or worse.

Emil Schnellock might well have been pardoned had he reacted to his friend's proclamation with a heavy dollop of skepticism. They'd known each other since they attended P.S. 85 in Brooklyn's Bushwick section some thirty years back, and for much of that time, it seemed, Miller had been jawing about becoming a writer. But after all the impassioned, profanity-spattered talk, some of it brilliant and colored with various violent prejudices; after his furious work on three extended pieces of fiction; after he'd left his first wife because a second one believed in his dream—after all this he had perilously little to show for it. The fictions remained unpublished and were perhaps unpublishable, and only a clutch of his shorter pieces had seen print in obscure places. Meanwhile, Schnellock, from a similar background and harboring his own artistic aspirations, had become a successful illustrator with a studio in Manhattan. What now could he have thought of his old friend, starving over there in Paris, except that once again Henry had failed? Maybe he also felt a little guilty, because it was he who had been partially responsible for

Miller's last-ditch, desperate decision to ship out for Paris in the winter of 1930, hoping the fabled city would somehow crack open that volcano of creative energy he felt he had within him. For Schnellock had seen Paris and the continent's other great cities and had for years been filling Miller with exquisitely detailed descriptions of those places and of that deep humus of art and culture so abundantly available there. Without quite meaning to he had encouraged in his friend a conviction amounting to a lifelong mania that America was hostile to artists, whereas the Old World was unfailingly nurturing. And when the desperate Miller, facing the death of his dream, and having really nowhere else to go, had decided it had to be Paris or bust, it had been Schnellock that he turned to, not his second wife June, who couldn't wait to be rid of him. Schnellock had put some steel in his spine and ten dollars in his pocket for the trip across the dark Atlantic and then down at the docks had seen him off.

Besides his ticket and Schnellock's tenner, Miller shipped with two valises and a trunk. In these he had some suits made by his tailor father, the drafts of two of the failed novels, and a copy of Walt Whitman's *Leaves of Grass*. But within him, buried beneath the accumulated detritus of a random and crudely assembled self-education, Miller was carrying a great deal more than these meager effects. In the lengthening years of his exile it became evident to him that his task was to discover through deprivation and doubt and often intense loneliness what this was that he carried and to learn how to make creative use of it.

From young manhood he had hated what his native land had become: more mercenary than the meanest whore and viciously intolerant of real or suspected deviations from the national norm. Such a phase in intellectual development, of course, is hardly unusual in young people in America and elsewhere in the developed world. But in Miller's case what he came to believe at so early an age he still believed on the last day he drew breath. Perhaps somewhat inchoate in his schoolboy years, this habit of mind was well established by the time he joined the workforce out of high school. By the time he shipped for Paris it was a pillar of his personality, a way of explaining where he now found himself, and the longer he was away from America, the more he hated it until the hatred became a hysteria that spattered the pages of his interminable letters to Emil Schnellock. When the war exiled him once again—back to America—he found his old home as hateful as ever and poured his feelings about it into such books as *The Air-Conditioned Nightmare* and its sequel, *Remember to Remember*, which invidiously compares America to *la belle France*. But if in 1930 he had imagined that Paris (and more generally the Old World) offered an authentic escape from the coarseness and heartlessness of America, he was wrong. Wrong about Henry Miller, anyway, because no one could have been in a certain sense more ineradicably American than the man who had left it on that wintry February morning. To be sure, he was definitely not a mainstream American, but still he belonged to a strong, colorful countervailing tradition of cranks, crooks, tall-talkers, hucksters, adventurers, outlaws, and utopian dreamers that had its roots deep in the American experience.

Even though his earliest associations were strongly flavored by his German ethnicity, once he had been loosed from his mother's apron strings he plunged headlong into the culture of his time and place, absorbing—almost helplessly it seems—its sights, sounds, smells, the rough roll of its urban rhythms, its prejudices and stunning contradictions. He was a great "noticer" of even the most minute details of quotidian life and could remember them years afterward. Much later he would elevate this talent to the status of a moral obligation. Thinking back to an old friend from the Paris days, Alfred Perlès, Miller invoked his injunction that the "mission of man on earth is to remember. To remember to remember." This is a great talent for a writer to have, of course, Marcel Proust being the prime example. Yet ungoverned it can become the enemy of coherence and form, leading him or her into distracting divagations and structural cul-de-sacs as well as endless back alleys of almost free association. Never one to deny himself the prompting of an instinct or the prospect of a pleasure, Miller characteristically followed whatever caught his interest, even if this was only fleetingly. "There was a child went forth every day," Walt Whitman wrote in 1855,

> And the first object he looked upon and received with
>   wonder or pity or
>   love or dread, that object he became,
> And that object became part of him for the day or a
>   certain part of the
>   day . . . or for many years or stretching cycles of years.

This was Henry Miller, who by 1930 had interested himself in various physical culture fads, burlesque theater, boxing, six-day bicycle races, professional wrestling, the production of chewing gum, the trade union movement, and radical politics; the cranks and toughs and petty criminals of his Brooklyn neighborhood; esoteric religious cults like theosophy; debating, tabloid journalism, the movies, and magicians. Also:

> American Can, American Tel. & Tel., Atlantic &
> Pacific, Standard Oil, United Cigars, Father John,
> Sacco & Vanzetti, Uneeda Biscuit, Seaboard Air Line,

Sapolio, Nick Carter, Trixie Friganza, Foxy Grandpa,
the Gold Dust Twins, Tom Sharkey, Valeska Suratt,
Commodore Schley, Millie de Leon, Theda Bara,
Robert E. Lee, Little Nemo, Lydia Pinkham, Jesse
James, Annie Oakley, Diamond Jim Brady, Schlitz-
Milwaukee, Hemp St. Louis, Daniel Boone, Mark
Hanna, Alexander Dowie, Carrie Nation, Mary Baker
Eddy, Pocahontas, Fatty Arbuckle, Ruth Snyder,
Lillian Russell, Sliding Billy Watson, Olga Nether-
sole, Billy Sunday, Mark Twain, Freeman & Clarke,
Joseph Smith, Battling Nelson, Aimee Semple
McPherson, Horace Greeley . . .

In *Black Spring* this list of public figures, place names, and
commercial products continues on until it reaches almost
two hundred. Such recollections of phenomena, however,
do not add up to artistic accomplishment. They are only
the potential raw materials of it. Still, the person on whom
little is lost (to use a variation of Henry James's notion of
the exemplary human being) is admirably positioned to
make creative use of what others have ignored or else have
regarded as the inevitable detritus of daily life.

This same omnivorousness had also played a role in
the lengthy list of occupations Miller had tried his hand at
by the time of his exile. He had been a file clerk, an agricultural laborer, a worker in a tailor shop—though he had

not actually been a tailor. For a brief time he worked in a bank, had taught piano, and had a stint as an editor at a mail-order catalog outfit. He ran a speakeasy with his second wife, June, and had been a handyman at a YMCA—though hazardously unhandy. He had sold encyclopedias door-to-door and chocolates to diners in Manhattan restaurants. For several years he had been an employment officer for Western Union. Most significantly from his point of view, he had tried writing, both as a freelance journalist and as an unsponsored freehand novelist whose models were the greats of continental literature.

Thus—and inevitably, as it must seem to us now—by 1930 Miller had willy-nilly absorbed so much of American culture, both past and present, that he could hardly have successfully escaped his nationality even had he fetched up somewhere in sub-Saharan Africa. Everything important about him reflected aspects of that very culture he never tired of disparaging. Like so many of his countrymen he was a shape-shifter, altering occupations, addresses, and personae as circumstances dictated. In a culture that historically had regarded a certain kind of lawlessness as a necessary virtue, Miller evidently felt more at home inhabiting a kind of murky fringe-land between a strict fidelity to the law and actual illegality, as if to be an outlaw of sorts was to be truest to the anarchical spirit that had gone into the making of a new nation. He was a tall-talker in a country that loved such talk and forgave a man much if only he had the "gift of gab." He was a man of pronounced, deeply held prejudices who, despite his parents' immigrant background, feared and disliked "foreign" newcomers as well as those who looked different from him. Seemingly almost from birth he believed in the natural superiority of men to women while remaining bewildered by the allegedly inferior gender's mysterious ability to reduce men to blobs of emotional jelly. While developing an authentic appreciation of the seven lively arts at their higher levels, Miller had a lot in common with those many Americans who spat on culture and hooted at its effeminate pretensions. Often for his profoundest pleasure he retreated to the crude humor of the barroom and the clubhouse, to literature at the level of the *Police Gazette*, and to burlesque, which was built on the mockery of high art. There was in him a broad comic streak, but as with so much of American humor there was almost always a shot of cruelty thrown in—sometimes a double. This special mixture—the American Grotesque—where laughter coexists with fear and suffering, high spirits with black despond—also characterizes Miller's personal temperament, which could veer from hilarity and cosmic optimism to the real blues and even suicidal despair.

Perhaps Miller's most significant connection to his culture was his unquenchable zest for adventure and improvisation, for it was this that had gone into exploration and settlement here; into technological innovation; into social experimentation on the grandest of scales; and into blues and jazz, those quintessential American art forms, which Miller sometimes emulated in his finest flights of prose. America, Miller believed, was improvisation itself writ large, and it was only when the nation turned away from that and began to calcify into a tyrannous orthodoxy that it betrayed its bright promise for the human race.

Aboard the *Bremen*, plowing eastward into the historic past, Miller felt himself in flight from all this—or as much of it as he could have been conscious of. America was now a "slaughterhouse" where millions were ground to gristle to feed the devouring maw of Progress. But over the ensuing months that would lengthen into years Miller was to learn that, while he might have escaped the slaughterhouse, he had not escaped the man America had shaped. In one of his letters to Schnellock he would claim that he was no longer an American, even if he wasn't a Frenchman and never would be. He was, he said with some justice, an expatriate. More precisely, though, what Miller had become was a renegade of a special sort.

The renegade of frontier history and folklore is driven by his hatred of the circumstances of his birth and upbringing, and this Miller certainly had in spades. But what he learned in Paris's bleakest quarters was that his background, his life and interests, his fund of knowledge of American history, folklore, and popular culture could be for him an inexhaustible source of creativity instead of a soul-withering curse. So, where too often the renegade comes to a violent and isolated end, Henry Miller not only survived, but bloomed into the artist he had so long—and apparently hopelessly—aspired to be. When at last in a foreign land he found his voice it was in a "war whoop," as he was to put it in *Tropic of Cancer.* The war whoop's raw notes were drawn from variegated sources. In part they came from the Yankee pitchman-bunco artist, a tale spinner who used his gift of gab to hoodwink his listeners. Another part of it came from the violently inflated brags of boatmen on the mighty rivers of the continental interior. There entered into it as well the bloody prints of the legends of deer slayers, buffalo hunters, backwoodsmen, Indian killers, and outlaws of the hinterlands and urban slums. Beneath all of these there was the brooding fact of discovery, the discovery of a vast, unexpected land mass that might have been an even greater opportunity to right the wrongs of the Old World's blood-wracked history— but was not. The war whoop that Miller sounds in *Tropic of Cancer* is fundamentally about this once-only chance. It consistently asks us in its rawness, its chaotic violence, its painful comedy, "What if?" Whitman, whose work he'd carried to France, had characterized his own belated breakthrough out of silence and stammering as a "barbaric yawp." That barbaric yawp had changed the national literature. Miller's war whoop was to do so again.

Slaughterhouse

If, as Miller claimed, America had become a slaughter-house, this condition had been centuries in the making, ever since, in fact, the Admiral of the Ocean Seas had first dropped anchor in 1492. Miller knew this, and his works are impressively studded with references to what began in that moment when Columbus's anchor hissed downward through unsullied waters. Miller recognized and was deeply affected by the tragically short arc there was between discovery and destruction, and far from the New World in the years of his exile the manifold consequences of this came into ever sharper relief. The great missed, unrepeatable opportunity that America had fleetingly been was eventually to become a major theme in *Tropic of Cancer.*

It is probably impossible to overestimate the profound implications of Columbus's accidental finding of the New World. This, of course, has been the subject of an uncounted number of books, and since the story is still being written in its unfolding chapters, the subject may truly be inexhaustible. Here it will have to suffice to observe that the admiral's epic blunder completely cracked open the mind of Western civilization, because in 1492 Christian cosmology posited a divinely created Island of the Earth surrounded by empty seas. If there were islands anywhere else—which most of the European continent's prominent thinkers doubted—these were bound to be tiny in size and uninhabited. The news, once disseminated, destroyed this portion of the myth, although the admiral himself stubbornly clung to the more comforting notion that what he had stumbled on was part of the Island of the Earth.[1] By around 1510 successive voyages by Alonso de Ojeda, Vicente Yáñez Pinzón, Rodrigo de Bastidas, and others had pretty well established that what Columbus had found was not a part of the Island of the Earth, at least as it had been anciently imagined, but was in fact another world, a New World, one that would somehow have to be accounted for and accepted.

But that acceptance came hard, very hard, and looking back over the more than five hundred years since Columbus made landfall it is difficult to ignore the feeling that

in the wake of that fateful October day it was as if an asylum in the Old World had been thrown open and hordes of vengeful madmen had been loosed upon the New. Here on these shores were men slashing and hacking at the natives, at the landscape, at each other with a frenzy that cannot be adequately explained by greed alone, though there was certainly plenty of that. Something more seemed at work, something that fueled the desire to almost instantaneously transform an inconvenient New World into a recognizable replica of the old one. Both the speed and the scale of the conquest were—and remain—astonishing and can never be replicated, on this planet, anyway, the Europeans swiftly overrunning and obliterating the native cultures, beginning with the empires of the Aztecs and Incas; then on to the seaboard tribes of North America; then the Six Nations of the Iroquois, the Five Civilized Tribes of the Old Southwest, the Plains tribes; and then on to the virtual extirpation of the California natives, down to the last, tiny remnant bands. In 1911, when the last "wild" California Indian emerged as a dazed, skeletal wanderer near Oroville in the north-central part of that state, some onlookers might well have wondered how it had all come down to just *this;* others, though, might just as easily have asked, "How did we miss this guy?

What was true of the assault on the natives was true as well of the New World's flora and fauna: forests leveled, streams desiccated, rivers diverted and dammed, animal habitats destroyed and whole species driven into extinction. All of this was most extravagantly apparent in North America, where there was a grim glee about the wholesale destruction, evident in successful communal efforts to wipe out wolves, mountain lions, the woods buffalo, martens, raccoons . . . Out of this history a spectral species of folk hero emerged in the figures of hunters who had racked up prodigious kill counts of this species or that. Buffalo Bill was the last and most famous of these figures but by no means the first. By his time his predecessors had long been forgotten (who remembers the celebrated panther killer, Aaron Hall?), but their deeds transformed a continent and left their bloody imprint on the American character. By 1911 when that lone Indian staggered into Oroville, the tribes had been transformed into beggars on reservations, and the once limitless herds of Plains buffalo had been pruned to an endangered few in Yellowstone Park, where they were hungrily eyed by hunters too young to have gotten in on all the fun. A continent, millennia in the making, had been transformed in four centuries.

A Great Beast

It could hardly be expected that a people capable of so astounding and reckless a transformation of the national landscape would prove solid, law-loving citizens of the fledgling democratic republic that emerged out of the American Revolution, and indeed they did not. From the end of the war to the simultaneous deaths of Thomas Jefferson and John Adams on Independence Day, 1826, the new nation was severely tested by threatened secessions; the anarchical tendencies of backwoods settlers and local militias who marched under the tattered standards of the "Wild Yankees," "Ely's Rebels," the "Paxton Boys," the "Black Boys," and the "Green Mountain Boys"; by numerous riots and lynchings; and by the rampant corruption of the democratic system. Surveying the political landscape in late 1786, George Washington told James Madison he thought the entire grand experiment might degenerate into "anarchy and confusion." And when the delegates from the states met in Philadelphia the following May for the Constitutional Convention they did so in the ominous shadow cast by Shays's Rebellion, which had come within an ace of success had the mutinous farmers taken the federal arsenal at Springfield. Not long thereafter new trouble bubbled up in Pennsylvania, eventually erupting in the Whiskey Rebellion in 1794, a more serious threat than Shays's Rebellion and with good reason: pioneer Americans drank whiskey all day long at a per capita rate of five gallons a year and would not brook an excise tax on what was for them meat and drink and a form of money.

There was another tax revolt in that same state in 1799. More serious still in its potential implications was Aaron Burr's murky plot that may have aimed ultimately at the dissolution of the Union. At the outset of the War of 1812 there were numerous antiwar protests, as well as violent demonstrations in support of it, including one in Baltimore where in June a mob destroyed the offices of the antiwar *Federal Republican*. When the paper tried to resume publication from a private house, that place was also attacked by superpatriots. On this occasion, Light Horse Harry Lee, hero of the Revolution (who had also fought against the insurgents in the Whiskey Rebellion) and who was defending the paper's right to publish, was so severely beaten by the mob that he eventually died of his injuries. More civil but more serious was the dissension evident at the Hartford Convention of 1815, which among other things challenged the very notion of a federal system that could appropriate customs money collected by the constituent states.

This turbulent history helps explain why Washington, Adams, Benjamin Rush, Fisher Ames, Alexander Hamilton, and others of the founding fathers viewed the American people as volatile and unruly, and why Hamilton is said to have called them a "great beast." Whether he actually said this or not, there is little doubt that he viewed his fellow citizens with alarm. At the Constitutional Convention he observed that the masses "are turbulent and changing: they seldom judge or determine right." Therefore, it was necessary that they be "sternly governed by the rich & wellborn"—not exactly a ringing endorsement of a democratic republic.

Perhaps no document surviving from the republic's early moments better preserves the striking contradictions between the radical idealism that fueled the founding of the nation and the violent, anarchical, racist tendencies lying beneath this than J. Hector St. John Crèvecoeur's *Letters from an American Farmer.* Well known in its author's lifetime, the book has enjoyed a sustained popularity ever since as a classic example of American idealism seen at its formative, generative roots. Here were stories of nameless immigrants who had come to these shores with nothing but pluck and who had swiftly prospered. Here were the fisherfolk of New England, bearing their hardships with a ruddy fortitude. Here were the yeoman farmers— God's chosen, as Jefferson had remarked—living lives of admirable simplicity and daily gratitude. And here too was that "fresh, green breast of the new world" (as F. Scott Fitzgerald was to put it in *The Great Gatsby*), a place of such inexhaustible plentitude as to seem positively paradisal to the newcomers. The American, Crèvecoeur writes in letter three, is in fact a new man, Adamaic in an unspoiled world and destined to carry the arts of industry ever westward, toward the gilded East that Columbus had vainly sought, and so complete the circle of human destiny.

It is true that the sustained popularity of *Letters* rests on Crèvecoeur's almost ecstatic evocation of America in the shining hour of its infancy. But there are darker tones here as well that speak of that baffled incredulity and vengeance that were the consequences of the unlooked-for finding of the New World, and Crèvecoeur had seen too much and was too honest to write only in praise. In the

American South where he was received by the gentry he saw the "peculiar institution" of slavery at work, and in the woods of South Carolina he stumbled upon a shocking scene—the punishment of an insubordinate slave—that called into the gravest question those egalitarian ideals that had gone into the making of the American Adam.[2] At that point in time the long-term consequences of this deep national contradiction could hardly, of course, have been apparent. But the contradiction itself was clear enough, and Crèvecoeur spoke it.

But more significant to him perhaps was the drama he knew firsthand, and this was the relentless advance of European-style civilization into the wilderness and what the implications of this might be. Thus, the most ringing, resonant sentence in *Letters* isn't the oft-anthologized one that begins, "*He* is an American, who leaving behind him," but instead the one that descends dramatically from the cloud-land of the *philosophes* to the American earth and the meeting of the furrowed with the forest: "Now we arrive near the great woods . . ."

In his travels—which took him as far west as the Great Lakes—Crèvecoeur had seen the ragged edges where the advance guard of white civilization met the wilderness and then camped uneasily there, and his extensive experiences conferred on him a unique understanding of the profound *wildness* that beat at the heart of the American experiment. Few knew how vast the country actually was or understood that the hardships of settling the eastern seaboard would have to be replicated in region after region in the westward push. What Crèvecoeur saw was that these hardships would become an enduring part of the national character, not merely a developmental stage. If you want to know what America is like (and what it will be like in future years), he writes, you "must visit our extended line of frontiers" where tiny settlements and solitary huts gave some shelter but little comfort to defalcators and drunkards, escaped criminals, runaway servants and slaves, half-hearted husbandmen who preferred the chase to the daily toil of cultivation, half-breeds and—worse—renegades who unnaturally turned against their own kind. Writing of the frontiersmen whom subsequent generations would deify, Crèvecoeur uses words like "hideous," "ferocious," "gloomy," "mongrel," and "half-savage"—and shudders to think of the consequences for America when such as these would serve as its pioneers and pass on to their children their violent and indolent habits. These people had quite naturally dreaded the inequities of the law in the Old World, he observed. But here in the New World where the law allegedly favored no class, they continued their anti-law habits of thought and behavior.[3] The best that could be hoped for was that in some long evolutionary process their sort would eventually disappear before the honest yeoman, as the sunlight of the plowed field replaced the gloom of the primeval forest.

Folklore of the Conquest

Out of the conquest of the continent and the subsequent growth of towns and cities there arose a folklore that, if it was not entirely indigenous, was strongly flavored by the national experience and the national character shaped by that. This was a folklore that celebrated the New England Yankee, the backwoodsman, boatmen of the heartland rivers; practical jokers, mighty liars, petty criminals and outlaws of the Old Southwest; and finally, legendary figures arising out of the shadows and slums of the cities.

The Yankee of folklore was essentially comic in nature, a dry-witted, slab-sided talker who, when he had risen from his oral origins to the almanac and the stage, was given to monologue. His wit cut sharply and was invariably at the expense of others, and before anybody could figure out who he was and what he was up to, he had vanished. His ability to change identities reflected something essential in the American experience and was not therefore ultimately limited to New England, for in this wooly, unformed New World a man might be required to play many roles.[4] He might have to change his name a few times, too, and when the relentless tide of westward advance had reached the new New World—California— there was a ditty about this particular habit:

> What was your name in the States?
> Was it Brown or Jackson or Bates?
> Did you murder your wife and fly for your life?
> Say, what was your name in the States?

The Yankee spun his tales, performed his sleights-of-hand, and changed his name and address, all with a blank, impenetrable mask behind which was—what? Maybe only a cunning collection of personae. He was so spare a figure that if you turned him sideways, he disappeared, leaving behind the puzzled victims who had bought the very last clock he had for sale. How much Miller knew of the doings of this folk figure is in question, but here as with the brawling backwoodsman and the outlaw the influences on him hardly need to have been direct: folk heroes arise because they represent repeated aspects of lived experience. Miller was no seller of clocks, but he had a good bit of the huckster in him and was certainly a changeable character, willing and able to alter guises as he needed to.

By contrast, the backwoodsman was so broad a character you couldn't miss him. He was clearly shaped by his hand-to-hand combat with the continent. That battle, as brutal and intimate as the gouging contests and naked knife fights that were his sports, made him boisterous, but also changeful of mood, instantaneously veering from Gargantuan celebration to slobbery sentimentality and then to a black and dangerous depression. You might say his character was humanity writ very large; or you might say he was hardly human at all, more bestial than manlike. This latter characterization would have been more to the character's own taste: you had to be more than a man to take on America: you had to be half horse, half alligator, as he was fond of describing himself. To an extent Daniel Boone was the historical figure this folk type was based on, a loner much more at home in the soaring solitude of the forest or the ominous density of the canebrakes than in white civilization with its crowdy ways. But the Boone of history was good for only a part of the backwoodsman's character. Something more was needed for that boisterous, boastful part, and for this the unnamed tale spinners turned to Davy Crockett, whom they embroidered into a high-hearted, heel-cracking hero who in some of his escapades approached a status almost mythic.

One morning, for instance, it was so preternaturally cold that the earth froze fast on its axis. So it was up to Crockett to pour on the grease from a fresh-killed bear to get creation cranked over again. When he gave the cosmic mechanism a kick-start, the

> sun walked up beautifully, salutin' me with sich a wind o' gratitude it made me sneeze. I lit my pipe by the blaze of his top-knot, shouldered my bear, an' walked home, introducin' people to the fresh daylight with a piece of sunrise in my pocket.

This character's style comes out of the antebellum period when the still-new nation was flexing its muscles and feeling its oats. It comes also out of a broader tradition of a people who just loved *talk*, talk for its own sake, for the sheer sound of it, the roll and pitch and the surprise of it when the magniloquent cadences were snapped short with some arresting turn of phrase or marvelously inventive folk metaphor. Of a man howling in pain, a Tennessee writer compared him to a "two-horse mowing-machine, driven by chain-lightning, cutting through a dry cane-brake on a big bet."[5]

A good deal of the backwoodsman got into the flatboatman figure of Mike Fink, celebrated for his feats on the Ohio and then on the Mississippi, and at last on no river at all except the nameless one that flows onward into oblivion. Fink partakes of something of Crockett's high style and Herculean powers. But his is a distinctly darker figure, one tinged with mayhem, murder, and alcoholism. To prove his marksmanship with a rifle he shoots the heel off a black man, the scalp-lock off an Indian, and countless cups of whiskey off the heads of his willing male cohorts. But there are times when Mike shoots for keeps, and a portion of his fame rests on his reputation as an Indian killer. Here he joins bloody heroes like Michael Cresap, a militia leader in western Maryland honored for slaughtering the family of the noted Mingo chief Logan; and Tom Quick of New York, who vowed to kill one hundred Indians before they got him but who died with only ninety-nine to his credit.

Eventually civilization spoiled Mike's sport: settlements now disfigured much of the Mississippi, and there was far less game. Maybe most importantly, there were fewer Indians to kill. Thomas Bangs Thorpe, one of the writers of the Old Southwest who wrote up some of that region's oral traditions, has Fink lamenting that, "Six months, and no Indian fights, would spile me worse than a dead horse on the prairie." With the old days of brawling and killing going or gone, there was little left for a man to do but to "turn nigger and work." No true hero would do that, and so Mike drifted westward ahead of the hordes. Somewhere out there, so a version goes, he proposed his familiar version of William Tell's trick, shooting a cup of whiskey from the head of his old friend, Carpenter. But this time Mike aimed a tad low, killing Carpenter. "Is the whiskey spilt?" Mike asked Carpenter's friend, Talbot. The question was over the line, even for this brand of humor, and not long thereafter Talbot saw his chance and avenged his late friend with Carpenter's own pistol.

In his unheroic death, Fink was succeeded by other breeds of folk figures, darker still, their legends almost unrelieved by any incidents of crude hilarity or comic boasts or heel-cracking hi-jinks. If there is any relief from the monochromatic mayhem of their stories, it is only that of the grim sort of humor engendered in the part of the Tom Quick legend telling how he finally got his hundred.[6] These newer figures were the land pirates of the Natchez Trace and the outlaws and gang members of New Orleans and New York who inhabited a new sort of frontier where the establishment of towns and the growth of cities provided tempting turf for those who lived in their shadows.

Of the former—the Natchez Trace land pirates—what their chronicler Robert M. Coates says of them can with justice serve as a characterization of this newer breed as a whole. They were, Coates writes, creatures of wilderness America, "the bitter fruit of the same wild seed that bred the pioneers: they reflected but in a more savage fashion, the same ruthless audacity and fierce implacable energy which its loneliness inspired in their more honest fellows."

The land pirates were the criminal consequence of the conquest of the eastern edges of the heartland, men who preyed on lone merchants traveling horseback along the Wilderness Road and the Natchez Trace, and also on the steadily swelling tide of boat traffic on the Mississippi. Some worked solo, others in small groups. And still others like Samuel Mason and John Murrel were said to operate gangs that in the successive retellings of their legends finally achieved the size of small armies. For all of them the work was hazardous, because every man out there went armed and frontier justice was rough, sometimes so much that its punishments almost beggared the crimes of the caught and convicted. In Tennessee, for instance, up until 1829 a convicted horse thief was branded on the right cheek with the letter H and on the left with a T. Then followed a public flogging. Finally, his ears were nailed to the pillory and cut off. This was for a first offense. Still, for the outlaws the rewards could be great, and in any case the work beat the sweat-of-the-brow labor of carving out a small farm and trying to make it support a family.

But some outlaws seemed to maraud merely for the pleasure it gave them, the homicidal maniacs the Harpe brothers being the most infamous example. "Big Harpe" (Micajah) and "Little Harpe" (Wiley) were technically robbers, but it might be that they really robbed so that they could have the greater satisfaction of murdering their victims. A shot in the back or a tomahawk to the head were their preferred methods, after which they would slit open the dead man's belly, fill it with rocks, and dump it into the river. When Big Harpe was mortally wounded by a pursuing posse in western Kentucky in 1799, one of the posse sawed off the dying outlaw's head while Big Harpe cursed him. "You are a God Damned rough butcher," he panted, "but cut on and be damned!"

Colonel Fluger, in some contrast, was interested in profits, though his method of making them was murder-by-the-boatload. Colonel Plug, as he was known, would slip aboard a boat, get down into its hold, and bore a hole in it. When the boat began to sink, Plug's companions, watching from shore, would row out to the rescue—but rescue only the goods, leaving the crew to drown. Eventually Plug was trapped belowdecks when a boat filled too quickly, and he went to the bottom with his victims.

The end of the outlaw chieftain Mason wasn't as neat as that of Plug or as savage as that of Big Harpe. Nevertheless, it has its characteristic frontier flavor. When a posse caught up with him west of Natchez, the pursuers tomahawked and decapitated him. Then, in order to claim the reward money, they covered the head in a ball of blue clay to prevent putrefaction and carried it to Natchez where it was duly identified.

Brawlers, outlaws, gamblers, filibusterers, land sharks, whores, runaway slaves—all these drifted on the Mississippi River's mighty sweep down to New Orleans. And there on its waterfront, in its cafés and coffeehouses, its high-roller casinos and splintered gambling dens, in its garishly appointed whorehouses and stinking one-room cribs there grew up a rich gumbo of oral traditions that persisted and multiplied long after print and the stage had pretty well choked off authentic folklore in regions where it once had flourished.

In New Orleans they told of the rough hordes of boatmen who would arrive there starved for women, whiskey, and fresh opponents to fight. And the town had everything they wanted, including the far-famed brawler Bill Sedley, who for years was more than a match for any upriver newcomer—but not for Annie Christmas, a six-foot-eight woman who could carry a flour barrel under each arm and a third one atop her head when she worked down on the docks. When she got bored with stevedoring, she would turn tricks down there until she'd worn her line of customers down to the last man. At other times she would transform herself into a one-woman towing machine capable of pulling a fully-loaded keelboat from New Orleans to Natchez on the dead run. Bill Sedley steered clear of Annie, and it was said she was also the reason Mike Fink stayed away from New Orleans. So one group's lore imaginatively overthrows another's.

The city's huge black population claimed Annie as its own and said she had twelve sons, each of them a seven-footer and coal black. But black and white, all New Orleans residents claimed the pirate king Jean Lafitte, who over the course of his career amassed a fortune by taking tall treasure ships in the Caribbean and running slaves up to the city from his base on Grand Terre. It was Lafitte and his pirates—Dominique You and Nez Coupé Chighizola, among others—who heroically came to General Andrew Jackson's aid at the battle of New Orleans that ended the War of 1812, and had it not been for them, the outcome, they say, would have been different.[7] Treated shabbily by the government he'd helped to save, the pirate king and his crew left America behind, sailing south. A few years later—off Mexico some said—he died in battle, leaving his treasure buried somewhere on Grand Terre where it lies undiscovered to this day.

Maybe only Macao was as given to gambling as New Orleans in the nineteenth century. Men would bet on anything and would bet everything, including all they owned—wives, slaves, plantations. The names of heroic gamblers like Star Davis, Jimmy Fitzgerald, Napoleon Bonaparte White, and Colonel Charles Starr were rolled off like a litany anywhere a form of chance took place— around a card table, out at one of the city's racetracks, in a cockpit, or at a dog fight. Jim McLane was among the most famous and a disgrace to his highly placed family: his mother sent him ten thousand dollars a year to stay away from home.

In 1938 the pioneering folklorist Alan Lomax chanced upon Jelly Roll Morton playing piano in a third-rate nightclub in Washington, D.C. By that point Morton was a prematurely aged and forgotten figure, but in the early years of jazz he was famous as a pianist, composer, and bandleader. And just as he could recall for Lomax the names and styles of men who played piano in the tonks of turn-of-the-century New Orleans—Sammy Davis, Alfred Wilson, Kid Ross, the incomparable Tony Jackson—so he could recall also the city's legendary gamblers, pimps, and outlaws of that time and place: Aaron Harris, Black Benny, Sheep Eye, Chicken Dick, and Ed Mochez who left behind a hundred and ten suits when he died. "Aaron Harris," Jelly told Lomax, "was no doubt the most heart-less man I've ever heard of. He could chew up pig iron— the same thing that would cut a hog's entrails to pieces— and spit it out razor blades."

There were heartless outlaws on the streets and water-fronts of New York, too, but in the nineteenth century they generally formed gangs, particularly after 1820, and there were times when they actually seemed to rule the entire city, as they did during the Draft Riots of July 1863. Slums like Five Points, the Bowery, and the Fourth Ward spawned gangs of such fearsome reputation as the Five Pointers, the Bowery Boys, the Plug Uglies, Dead Rabbits, and the Hudson Dusters. They fought each other for turf and for control of certain forms of commerce and roughneck entertainment, sometimes in pitched battles that would go on for days. Figures like Mose, the "Bow-ery B'hoy," whatever their historical origins may have been, transcended the grim and doubtless pathetic facts of their lives to become legends and at last the sanitized figures of popular culture. At the level of oral lore Mose was an eight-foot figure of terror, carrying into battle a ponderous paving stone in one hand and a wagon tongue in the other. If an opponent was lucky enough to avoid these, Mose might stomp him to death with his copper-soled shoes studded with inch-long nails. His Herculean habits recall in an urban vein those of young Mike Fink: in the dog days of summer Mose was to be seen striding the mean streets of his kingdom with a fifty-gallon keg of ale swinging from his belt. By the 1840s and thereafter

Mose became a comic figure of the stage, a swaggering, flag-waving tall-talker in a red flannel undershirt.

Equally fiercesome if not gigantic was George Leese, better known as Snatchum, a member of the Slaughter House gang, who prowled the waterfront dripping with his weaponry. His singular claim to fame, though, was his work at bare-knuckle boxing matches where Snatchum acted as a kind of precursor of modern-day boxing's expert "cut men." But Snatchum, instead of cauterizing and swabbing the boxers' cuts, as the modern men do, would suck the blood from their wounds. Others in the pantheon with him included Hop Along Peter, Patsy Conroy, Kid Shanahan, Kid Twist, and the original Billy the Kid, a thief who was arrested one hundred times before his twenty-sixth birthday. Big Nose Bunker belongs here as well. Big Nose was a celebrated rough-and-tumble fighter whose final opponent chopped off four of his fingers and stabbed him six times in the stomach. Somehow Big Nose was able to carry his fingers in a paper sack to the nearest police station where he asked for a doctor to sew them back on. He died before the ambulance arrived.

Twain

The Deerslayer, American fiction's first major character, is an oblique and somewhat sanitized reference to America's dark and violent past. But very little else of this folk-based material entered the national literature's mainstream until the career of Mark Twain, and none of it in all its hairy violence, its cruel humor, its profanity, sexuality, casual bigotry, and xenophobic contempt for anything foreign or smacking of culture (often enough regarded as synonymous). As for language, the American vernacular was confined to levels far beneath polite letters. It appeared in minstrel shows, in newspaper sketches, and in almanacs that mingled jokes and regional speech oddities with crop forecasts and reports of three-headed calves. It appeared also in burlesque, which achieved enormous popularity after the Civil War, especially in New York City. But even in burlesque, with its bawdiness and disdain for just about everything, the full dimensions of the vernacular were hardly more than hinted at, as if in the broad innuendo, the double entendre, the smutty stage whisper audiences were being invited to understand and participate in an otherwise forbidden code. Beyond this there was nothing to indicate the liberal profanity, the crude sexuality that must certainly have been there in the stories swapped about Mike Fink, Annie Christmas, Big Harpe, even Crockett, whose comic antics and speech would originally have been strong stuff indeed at the oral level.

In his famous Phi Beta Kappa address at Harvard in 1837, "The American Scholar," Ralph Waldo Emerson had boldly called for a literature that would reach down to the real roots of the American experiment and speak in a radically native way. "Give me," he said,

> the insight into to-day, and you may have the antique and future worlds. What would we really know the meaning of? The meal in the firkin; the milk in the pan; the ballad in the street; the news of the boat. . . .

But what could the Concord sage have known of the news of the boat when that boat was a keelboat or a broadhorn docking at the noisome slum of Natchez-under-the-Hill

or New Orleans where some eighty years later a preco-
cious Jelly Roll Morton was learning the street songs that
would ultimately scorch the stately décor of the Library
of Congress's Coolidge Chamber Music Auditorium when
he recorded them for Alan Lomax? Henry Miller would
have loved this stuff. Emerson would have been appalled.
Nor could he have imagined the existence of unlettered
artists of profanity who could reduce their audiences to
stunned silence with their long, rolling braids of oaths and
epithets—rude oral-formulaics such as those that made
possible the Homeric epics. Emerson was perhaps our
most original thinker, and at great effort he had struggled
out of the heavy cloak of his ancestral Puritanism to en-
courage American writers and artists to create art out of
the experiences of a new world instead of pining for those
of an old one. He had, however, a thin opinion of fiction
(including that of his neighbor, Nathaniel Hawthorne)
and thought that eventually "these novels" would give
way to truer and more serious stuff. And he actually never
learned much about the life of the street or the waterfront
and even less about what went on where the ragged edges
of civilization met the great woods—certainly far less than
Crèvecoeur. Lecturing in Beloit, Wisconsin, in the winter of 1856 where it was twenty below, he confided to his
journal that he knew well enough that his rough audience
in their thawing coats and boots could accept his wisdom

only if it came in comic dress. But he couldn't give them that. Wit he had, though he employed it sparingly. But not that comic spirit that kept company with violence to make up the American Grotesque.

Emerson saw more of the country than Henry Thoreau did, though almost always surrounded by Bostonian acolytes who did their best to shield him from certain incivilities. But on the wild shores of Cape Cod and in those great woods Crèvecoeur had written of, Thoreau learned things about America that his mentor had at best but intuited. It wasn't only the remaining wilds of the east, as in Maine, that inspired his observation that there was still a lot of America that remained undiscovered. It was as well that unconquerable wildness beating in America's heart. It made the nation coarse, uncouth, and at times even disgusting to him. How it would ever get into literature as he understood that term was a question. What would the literature be like if someone like his Indian guide in Maine, Joe Polis, learned to read and write? As for his own work, when he chose, Thoreau could write close to the vernacular, employing here and there certain of its pithy and colorful terms, but for him that was more than enough flavoring. His themes were after all relentlessly lofty and required an appropriate diction.

When he went down to New York to meet Whitman in

1856, he seemed almost to shrink from too close a contact with this self-styled "rough" who appeared positively to glory in phenomena so decidedly anti-poetic: the sounds of boot soles on the city's pavements, the talk of boatmen and clam diggers around a chowder pot. Who wrote as well of

Arrests of criminals, slights, adulterous offers made,
    acceptances, rejections with convex lips . . .

And then there were passages like this one that could not but have horrified a man who was always striving to overcome the inconvenience of having been born with a body that had its own needs:

I mind how we lay in June, such a transparent summer
    morning;
You settled your head athwart my hips and gently turned
    over upon me,
And parted the shirt from my bosom-bone, and plunged
    your tongue to my barestript heart,
And reached till you felt my beard, and reached till you
    held my feet.

To his great credit, Thoreau fought past his squeamishness to recognize the poet's singular power and authenticity, that what Whitman was writing pointed the way the literature of a democracy would have to go, even if he couldn't go there himself. He was profoundly in the American grain—but always somehow a little bit above it: he would not write of the city's wharves and docks and crowds, nor yet of tipsy prostitutes with pimpled necks or of bloody suicides sprawled in some tenement room with the pistol beside the body. He did want to see the Great West and write about it, but he didn't live long enough.

It took American writers about sixty years to begin to appreciate what Whitman had done in the first three editions of *Leaves of Grass,* and even well after that Henry Miller could with real justice refer to Whitman as that "rude hieroglyphic," so astonishingly modern was his work. But the literary impact of Mark Twain was immediately apparent. Here in ink and on paper and available at polite levels of the culture was America *talking*—not writing—in the outsized, colorful monologue mode that had been a century and more in the making. After Twain's long career had come to an end, his old friend the novelist and editor William Dean Howells called him the "Lincoln of our literature." The tribute stuck, though it is not clear just what Howells meant by it. Many things maybe. Clearly he meant that his friend was unlike any writer who'd come before him—"sole, incomparable." Maybe he also meant to draw comparisons between the two men from the heartland who had known the great rivers, their life and lore. And just as Lincoln had drawn on the jokes and stories of that region for his own jokes, illustrative comparisons, and metaphors, so for everything that was best in his writing Twain drew from frontier, folk-based materials. It is also possible that Howells may have been thinking that as Lincoln had freed the slaves, so Twain had freed American literature from its slavish devotion to Anglo-European models and taught it to admire the sound of its own voice, endlessly gabbing and tale-spinning.

When Twain got up on his hind legs in *The Innocents Abroad* (1869), having swiftly outgrown his reputation as merely a western funny man, it was clear that his was a voice that defiantly spoke American lingo and wasn't shy about making fun of the Old World and everything that went with it. That the fun was as ignorant as it was crude was what in fact made it so funny to his countrymen, with their well-established bias against culture as effeminate foolishness. Twain played to this audience relentlessly in *Innocents*, portraying himself and his fellow travelers "galloping" through the Louvre, the Pitti, and all the rest of the continent's great museums, glancing quickly at the "modern and ancient statuary with a critical eye in Florence, Rome, or any where we found it, and we praised it if we saw fit, and if we didn't we said we preferred the wooden Indian in front of the cigar stores of America."

Then there were the Old World's heaps of religious relics, which proved to be a mother lode of laughs for an American armed with Twain's savage sense of humor, about the verbal equivalent of a six-shooter:

> We find a piece of the true cross in every old church we go into, and some of the nails that held it together. I would not like to be positive, but I think we have seen as much as a keg of these nails. Then there is the crown of thorns; they have part of one in Sainte Chapelle, in Paris, and part of one, also in Notre Dame. And as for the bones of St. Denis, I feel certain we have seen enough of them to duplicate him, if necessary.

There is something very democratic—in one sense of the term—about the broad-gauge scale of the slander here: everything gets it. Everyone gets it as well: Portuguese, Italians, North Africans, the French, Turks, even some California Indians when Twain can't find any handier targets. Comparing Italy's Lake Como with California's Lake Tahoe, Twain is reminded that "Tahoe"

> means grasshoppers. It means grasshopper soup. It is Indian and suggestive of Indians. They say it is Pi-ute—possibly it is Digger. I am satisfied it was named by the Diggers—those degraded savages who

roast their dead relatives, then mix the human grease and ashes of bones with tar, and "gaum" it thick all over their heads and foreheads and ears, and go caterwauling about the hills and call it *mourning*.

Such sentiments as these make it easy enough to understand how it came to pass that in 1911 that lone "wild" Indian in Oroville could have been regarded as such an anachronistic curiosity.

Twain's great subject, of course, was the river on the banks of which he grew up. When he turned back to it imaginatively in the summer of 1874, he had entered his major phase, the one that did so much to make him the Lincoln of our literature. Two years thereafter he published *The Adventures of Tom Sawyer*, which along with *Life on the Mississippi* (1883) and *The Adventures of Huckleberry Finn* (1884) constitute his finest work. In these books Twain was able to portray, brilliantly, American culture in all its cantankerous vitality in a way that hadn't been done before: not by the regionalists like Seba Smith or Johnson J. Hooper or George Washington Harris; nor by the greats of the American Renaissance, Emerson, Thoreau, Hawthorne, Herman Melville. Whitman came very close, but after the first three editions of *Leaves*, he unaccountably began to veer off toward Literature with a capital L, as if he felt he had stuck his neck out too far, been too radically American, and now had to retreat in the direction of safer models.

Twain, on the other hand, was closer than any of his illustrious predecessors to the oral traditions that had grown up with the country. They were in some important sense all the education he would ever need, but like many of his countrymen he held a wide variety of jobs where he picked up additional imaginative capital: printer's devil, river pilot, Civil War recruit, prospector, journalist, and lecturer. In these guises he'd encountered a broad spectrum of certain American realities that earlier important authors hadn't—or else had decided to ignore. Only Melville's wealth of experience comes anywhere close.

Though apparently from youth somewhat bookish, Twain knew how strong the anti-literary strain was in the culture, and it appears in his best books where the authorial stance is one in which the writer implicitly says to the reader, "*Listen:* I'm not a writer like those other fellows. I'm a tale-teller, and my books are really yarns." In *Huckleberry Finn*, his finest achievement, this stance is made explicit when Twain adopts the literary persona of an ignorant boy who disowns the man who had written about him in *Tom Sawyer* because that man was a writer, and writers can't tell the truth. The truth Huck tells us is of a voyage down the country's main artery into its violent heart, a home to criminals and child abusers, blood feuds and mob violence, and to the historic trafficking in human flesh. At the end of that voyage—which is also a yarn—the boy who has seen it all tells us that he's seen enough, that he wants to light out for the Territory "ahead of the rest." This impulse, as Crèvecoeur had earlier observed, was the American story, the yarn the country itself had spun and had permanently captivated itself in the spinning of it.

Huck tells us he's told the truth here. But had he, or had his creator prevented him from telling all that he had seen, all that he had heard? Was there yet another layer of truth that had been left unsaid?

In writing *Life on the Mississippi* from recollections, personal notes, news clippings, source books, old timetables, Twain also appropriated a passage from a manuscript he had shelved some years before and used it as the basis for a chapter he called "Frescoes from the Past." The shelved manuscript was *Huckleberry Finn*, and what Twain now saw was that he could put it to use here to give his readers the full flavor of the Mississippi's life as he had come to know it as a boy, a cub pilot, and at last as a fully fledged pilot himself. To set it up, he gives us this description of the men of the Mike Fink era:

> rude, uneducated, brave, suffering terrific hardships
> with sailor-like stoicism; heavy drinkers, coarse

frolickers in moral sties like the Natchez-under-the-hill of that day, heavy fighters, reckless fellows, every one, elephantinely jolly, foul-witted, profane; prodigal of their money, bankrupt at the end of their trip, fond of barbaric finery, prodigious braggarts; yet in the main, honest, trustworthy, faithful to promises and duty, and often picturesquely magnanimous.

The steamboat, Twain continues, put such men out of business, forcing them to become deckhands or else raftsmen on the huge pine-board carriers that swept past riverfront hamlets like Hannibal in mighty procession, "all managed by hand, and employing hosts of the rough characters whom I have been trying to describe." It is a telling remark, this effort to describe such rough characters. In the social and literary culture of the East to which he had so successfully laid siege, Twain now found himself faced with the task of somehow rendering in print "the rude ways and the tremendous talk" of the crews, "the ex-keelboatmen and their admiringly patterning successors; for we used to swim out a quarter or a third of a mile and get on these rafts and have a ride." Then comes the passage lifted from *Huckleberry Finn* in which Twain gives us a sample of that "tremendous talk" where a man might advertise his dangerous character by claiming to be the old original iron-jawed, brass-mounted, copper-bellied corpse-maker from the wilds of Arkansaw!—look at me! I'm the man they call Sudden Death and General Desolation! Sired by a hurricane, dam'd by an earthquake, half-brother to the cholera, nearly related to the small-pox on the mother's side! Look at me! I take nineteen alligators and a bar'l of whiskey for breakfast when I'm in robust health, and a bushel of rattlesnakes and a dead body when I'm ailing!

Brilliant stuff here in which the writer packs into this formulaic comic boast not only Mississippi River lore but really a century of the American experience with its violence, its color, its astonishing vitality.

But Twain sets himself an even greater challenge when two chapters later he tries to reproduce the daily language of the men who worked the gaudy steamboats. Formulaic comic boasts were one thing, but the ordinary language of a workday spent on the docks and decks under all kinds of conditions was another, for these men were the cultural descendants of those Twain had said were the coarse, foul-witted, profane frolickers who haunted the river's "moral sties." He remembered—or claimed to—a particular mate from his own days as a cub pilot, a great, stormy fellow with a blue woman tattooed on one arm and a red one on the other and who was a genuine artist in his command of profanity. When this man gave an order, Twain tells us, "he discharged it like a blast of lightning, and sent a long, reverberating peal of profanity thundering after it." For example: "'Aft again! aft again! Don't you hear me? Dash it to dash . . . !'" And, "'you dash-dash-dash-*dashed* split between a tired mud-turtle and a crippled hearse horse!'" This leaves a considerably less pungent impression than do the comic boasts, because here the attempt to portray the everyday realities of river life runs aground on the social and literary realities Twain had come to know so well. There were many things that simply couldn't be written in literature, even if they were the commonplace realities of American life.

It could well be argued—and doubtless has been—that literature is the better for these prohibitions, that there is nothing artful at all in giving readers the real words the tattooed mate might have used on his deckhands, because such words could only be the crude verbal clubs such a man would have had at hand, as a man in a brawl might grab whatever weapons there were—hatchet, cudgel, bottle. But we are obliged to remember here Twain's strong anti-literary, anti-establishment bias, plus the fact that in writing about the river he was writing about the thing he loved more than anything else in life, except possibly his family.

First and last, Twain's literary persona and thus his financial success depended on the popular perception of him as a kind of outlaw who had—somehow—learned to wear a cravat and to read and write. And this wasn't all a pose, either: there were several notable instances in which Sam Clemens went far out of his way to antagonize members of the so-called "Genteel Tradition," as when he savagely mocked Emerson, Oliver Wendell Holmes, and Henry Wadsworth Longfellow as they sat at the head table at the birthday dinner for John Greenleaf Whittier in 1877. And as for the river and its life, what Twain must surely have yearned to do was to give his readers the authentic, one-hundred-proof, forty-rod stuff he knew—language, behavior, and all. We need to take him seriously when he says after attempting to reproduce the tattooed mate's profane outburst, "I wished I could talk like that." He could—in private—up in his dressing room, in the bathroom, or down at the billiards table where a missing shirt button, a dull razor, or a bad shot would cause him to break out his own formidable arsenal of words and expressions he'd picked up on the river.

Not in print, though, with the single exception of the privately circulated story "1601," which purported to be an account of conversation around Queen Elizabeth's fireside in which Her Majesty endeavors to learn who it was among Shakespeare, Ben Jonson, Francis Bacon, Sir Walter Raleigh, and others who had blown a terrific fart. The exercise is rather a pathetic one, both inherently and considering the schoolboy glee with which it was received, praised, and passed around by Twain's circle of socially prominent male friends. If it has any virtue, it is that it serves to suggest the power of the regnant literary prohibitions and beneath these the force of that current of sub-literary reality that had been flowing through American life for more than a century.

It is in this context that the last notebook entry Twain ever made takes on resonance. It is the single word, "*Talk.*" And it was a certain sort of talk—rough, uncensored, a brilliantly sustained monologue—that would have to await utterance until the obscure advent of another literary outlaw, a renegade really, willing to risk everything to talk about life as he saw it in language that adequately expressed his vision. One had to go back to Christopher Marlowe and Shakespeare, Norman Mailer wrote of Henry Miller, to find a writer of such startling intensity, of such artistic audacity.

Just a Brooklyn Boy

For a writer who was so compulsively autobiographical and who for the last half century of his life saved or made copies of much of what he wrote, it is surprising how many facts of Miller's life are either unknown or in dispute. We are not even certain of the original spelling of the family name—whether in the Old World the paternal line had it Mueller or Müller or Muller before Anglicizing it to Miller on coming to America.

The major problem here is Miller himself, who was as compulsive a mythologizer as he was autobiographical, incessantly and even gleefully inventing competing versions of events and further elaborating on some of these, so that what he left behind at his death was a vast palimpsest presenting biographers and critics with a plethora of problems that can never be definitively solved. The problems are particularly acute for the pre-Paris years, where we have little really substantial to go on *except* Miller. Here one is forced to the hazardous expedient of using his later reconstructions of characters and events, knowing full well that these are reconstructions—when they are not pure inventions. At least, however, we are here in the realm of imaginative truth, which for Miller himself was truer than true.[8]

This much at least is certain: Heinrich (later Henry) Miller and Louise Nieting were both children of German immigrants who had two children of their own, Henry (1891) and Lauretta (1895). When Henry was less than a year old the family moved from Yorkville in Manhattan across the river to the Williamsburg area of Brooklyn, the Fourteenth Ward, which Miller would later recall with an intensity that produced some of his most colorful work. These earliest years were passed inside the kind of hermetical immigrant enclosure possible in those days before the mass media, mass transit, and mass production had combined to homogenize the national culture. In the Miller-Nieting household on Driggs Avenue the child heard mostly German and spoke his first words in that language. The food was German, the next-door neighbors were German, and the large frame of daily reference was Germany, not America. And despite a determinedly vagabond existence and the global range of his interests and enthusiasms, there were certain things about Miller that remained forever German.[9] When his personal circumstances permitted, for example, he preferred the neat and orderly household of his childhood, one where things were put away after they were used, where floors were swept and counters wiped clean. In his Paris days, when he could afford a substantial meal, he was likely to seek out a German restaurant or at least an Alsatian one like Zeyer or Wepler in the Place de Clichy. There were less obvious preferences, too, that bespoke his ethnic heritage. Behind the helter-skelter, improvisational nature of his maturity there was a dogged search for some ordering, synthesizing principle that would make comprehensive sense of chaos, calling to mind that strong tradition of Germanic philosophers of history—Immanuel Kant, Wilhelm Dilthey, Theodor Mommsen, Ernst Haeckel, Karl Marx, and especially Oswald Spengler, a high god in Miller's pantheon. Yet once he had gotten beyond what he characterized as his period of intellectual stammering, a part of Miller turned against his background with a ferocity that tells us how deep it really went with him. "My people were entirely Nordic," he would write in *Tropic of Capricorn*, "which is to say, *idiots*. They were painfully clean. But inwardly they stank."

After dinner the dishes were promptly washed and put in the closet; after the paper was read it was neatly folded and laid away on the shelf; after the clothes were washed they were ironed and then tucked away in drawers. Everything was for tomorrow, but tomorrow never came.

According to her son, this mindless mania for order was the work of his mother. On the other hand, the father, a master tailor who ran his own shop, was in many respects a Good Time Charlie who loved his beer and his boon companions and who over the years of Miller's adolescence and young manhood became a gentle alcoholic. Whatever her original nature may have been, Louise was quite a different sort by the time Miller was able to remember her behavior. Mental illness ran on her side of the family (Lauretta inherited it), and from an early age it had fallen to Louise to create what semblance of normality there could be in her family's household. The habit carried over into her marriage, and the couple was badly mismatched, ever more so as Henry Senior slid into alcoholism and began to neglect his business. Miller claimed that it wasn't until he himself had reached the age of fifty that he was able to summon up a single affectionate thought about Louise, and however this may be, it doesn't take overmuch psychologizing to wonder whether some of his treatment of women, both in life and in art, owes something to his attitude toward the brooding shadow of this authoritarian figure. It was she, he once claimed, who planted the demon of rebellion in his soul at an early age, because whatever he might be doing, he always felt her disapproval.

As if he were watching the world exclusively from the living room window or the steps of the house on Driggs, the small boy's earliest memories were of the immediate surroundings and the resident odors: the fish house next door; the neatly kept house and yard of the German neighbors on the other side; the tin factory whose smoke-blackened laborers appeared to him as slaves in hell; the smells of the tanyard, the gas mains, and the dung and urine of the workhorses.

When he went outside it was always in the company of his mother who kept him firmly in hand, a practice that continued well after his contemporaries had graduated to a greater freedom. But inevitably, even a monster of control such as he represented Louise to have been would have to let go, allowing little Henry to begin his own explorations of his Williamsburg world. And if in the beginning that world would have seemed to him exclusively German, he was soon to find that it was in fact a rich and gamy ethnic stew with strong flavorings of Irish, Italians, Poles, Scandinavians, Syrians, and, increasingly as the century came to a close, eastern European Jews. On street corners and in vacant lots; in vest pocket parks and down at the docks; on the sidewalks outside saloons, butcher shops, the veterinarian's office, and a burlesque theater known as "The Bum," where Millie de Leon drove grown men mad, the boy was quickly toughened up. He learned techniques of self-defense, what it took to fit in, taking on the protective coloration of the corner cliques and the neighborhood gangs. He got his first black eye from a tough Mick named Eddie Carney. With a few cronies he caught a glimpse of a little girl's private parts and watched the vet geld a stallion. Outside the saloons he inhaled the heady perfume of beer, sawdust, and tobacco smoke, and learned what drunkenness looked like.

Williamsburg was filled with folkloric personalities, and the more colorful they were, the more outrageous, violent, even deranged, the more the boy was drawn to them. There were characters like Apple Annie and Clarence the Cop who were just that—characters who could have no other dimensions to them for the boy. Others he knew better, like Crazy Willie who barked like a dog and masturbated in public. There were also the tough guys—the sports—who swaggered through their world of the "saloon, the race track, bicycles, fast women and trot horses," as he was later to style it. His personal roster of these folk heroes included Stanley Borowski, Matt Owen, the great Johnny Paul, and Lester Reardon, "who, by the mere act of walking down the street, inspired fear and admiration." And there were Rob Ramsay and Jack Lawson. Rob Ramsay came back from the war covered with decorations, and then soon enough covered himself with his own drunken vomit until one fine day in an act of supreme herohood he walked off the end of a pier and drowned himself. Of Jack Lawson we know only that when Miller was twelve this best of friends died of some unspecified illness and that Miller was so glad Jack was now out of his misery that he claims he "let a loud fart" right beside the coffin where Jack's relatives were "bawling like sick monkeys."

There were no heroic figures in Miller's family, but a fair share of mental defectives and misfits, beginning with Lauretta, who never developed intellectually much past the level of a ten-year-old. Louise's desperate efforts to browbeat an education into her daughter were a continuing source of anguish to Miller, who was often a helpless witness to them. Somewhere in this protracted, painful process he developed a coping technique that would become an essential part of his character: when his mother's efforts at home-schooling Lauretta would reach a hysterical level and the slapping started, he would make some sort of inward, imaginative escape to a place where the slaps and Lauretta's frightened outcries weren't present any longer and the boy was impervious and indifferent to the suffering there in front of him.

In his maturity he was never able to make these scenes between mother and daughter seem comic, something he was able to do with so much other unpromising family material. But the rest of the family became, quite literally, another story, and in his cruelly hilarious recollections of them we hear the distant echo of such folk figures as Mike Fink asking whether the whiskey cup had been spilled after killing his friend Carpenter. Confronted with what he came to regard as the crowd of freaks and halfwits that made up his family tree, Miller created out of chaos and failure, illness and insanity, a group portrait that is funny in the way the grotesque is funny—at considerable cost. Among those who got together on almost any occasion, he wrote in *Black Spring*, there was

> cancer, dropsy, cirrhosis of the liver, insanity, thievery, mendacity, buggery, incest, paralysis, tapeworms, abortions, triplets, idiots, drunkards, ne'er-do-wells, fanatics, sailors, tailors, watchmakers, scarlet fever, whooping cough, meningitis, running ears, chorea, stutterers, jailbirds, dreamers, storytellers, bartenders. . . . The morgue and the insane asylum.

Despite all, it was amazing how jolly this pitiful group could be, regardless of the weather (whether it was zero or below) or the circumstance (a death, the outbreak of another war, or the tin factory catching fire again). There they were, laughingly gathered around the festive table crammed with "sauerkraut with kartoffelklöze and sour black gravy . . . with apple sauce and figs from Smyrna, with bananas big as blackjacks," everything except a finger bowl.

Neither in his extended family nor in the little unit of it living on Driggs were there any who were actively involved in the arts, though Louise had once played a couple of musical instruments, and Henry himself learned to play the piano passably. Paintings were scarce around the house as were books, except in Henry's room. Very early he showed a bookish inclination that his parents indulged with gifts of *Robinson Crusoe*, G. A. Henty—the boys' favorite of that era—H. Rider Haggard, and *The Adventures of Pinocchio*, whose besetting sin was his chronic lying. But if neither Henry Senior nor Louise were readers, museumgoers, or much interested in serious theater, still they had an Old World respect for culture. The arts were a good thing, and they knew that many great writers had written in their native tongue, even if they themselves had never read them. They knew also how important it was that they themselves master the new tongue of their world, and in their household they had the example of Grandpa Nieting, who spoke the beautiful English he'd learned in London on his way to America. Because of this he was a respected member of Brooklyn's German-American community.

As for little Henry, once he had been sprung from the household with its German language and customs, he quickly became adept at the gutter talk of Williamsburg. This must have been pretty rough stuff, because when an older girl happened to hear him using it she was so shocked she collared him and dragged him off to the police station. This might have been the first time his use of language got him in trouble with the law, though it certainly was not the last.[10]

Beginning the Streets of Sorrow

These early years, Miller was to recall ever afterward, were ones in which he was having a grand time because he "really didn't give a fuck about anything." By this he apparently meant that he was yet young enough that no one expected him to have a goal in life. But the interesting thing here is that what Miller recalled of himself at about the age of eight was really what he said of himself near the end of his life when he was a living legend who could say that if his fame had permitted it, he would do nothing, "and I mean absolutely nothing." While his sister remained forever locked in early childhood by her mental illness, Miller himself, though quite bright, remained forever in certain important respects a kind of Huck Finn character whose goal in life was to avoid growing up, to avoid as much as possible what the world called "work" and "responsibility," so that he might live a life of anarchical freedom in some mental territory beyond the reaches of civilization. He never saw himself "getting ahead," laboriously climbing the steep way to success as his world commonly measured it. Instead he wanted to follow his own path, and that path led always away from the beaten one, the one that America had cut with such fabulous speed and energy and now was hell-bent on pointing out to the rest of the world.

This sort of indolent insouciance became harder for the boy to carry off when he was only nine, at which point his family decided Williamsburg was changing for the worse with the steady influx of Italians and eastern European Jews. His parents wanted to find a more stable, homogeneous German-American neighborhood and found it in Brooklyn's Bushwick section in 1900. Here was a body blow to little Henry, ending what he always felt was an urban idyll he would have been happy to have lived endlessly. The new neighborhood represented new challenges for him and new gangs whose tribal rituals he would have to learn, beginning on the day a kid placed a chip on the newcomer's shoulder, meaning he would have to fight or be ostracized. Instead, Miller told the other kids that he knew none of them and therefore had nothing against them. There was nothing for him to fight about, he said.

Apparently his stance was sufficiently peculiar to buy him amnesty, and he was accepted as an eccentric—precisely the sort of character that appealed to Miller himself. This, however, didn't affect his homesickness for Williamsburg; he missed the old neighborhood with a deep poignancy and would always refer to the new house on Decatur Street as the "street of early sorrows."

At P.S. 85 he was regarded as a good student, though often bored and therefore mischievous. He didn't have to work hard at all to master the rote learning he was assigned and had plenty of time to continue his own unsupervised reading. He made a close friend of Emil Schnellock, whose draftsmanship everyone admired, including the teacher who often asked Emil to come forward to draw on the blackboard. Here was a form of distinction new to Miller: maybe you didn't have to be a tough guy, a rock thrower, a street fighter, to stand out. Maybe you could use your imagination. Yet when it came time to move on to high school, Miller chose to leave Emil and the others behind, going back to Williamsburg and its Eastern District High.

He found the old neighborhood much changed, just as his family had feared. There were now a great many more Jews than he'd remembered, so many in fact that he and his kind were outnumbered, an unpleasant situation for him that gave rise to a persistent, virulent anti-Semitism that later he would try to disguise as a form of envy, even going so far as to suggest that there must have been Jewish blood in his own lineage. To an extent, however, Miller's anti-Semitism needs to be seen in a larger cultural context. What now might be regarded as bigotry and unacceptable ethnic slurring was then a common and historic fact of American life, and if it was not present at the very outset of the American experiment, this was only because immigration from places other than the British Isles was not yet the huge phenomenon it was to become. "Mick," "kraut," "dago," "polack," "chink," and so on were casually employed by adults and their children. "Nigger" and "kike" were used as well, but these latter terms, while they continued to be common at the street level, gradually dropped from acceptable usage.[11] Miller continued to use "nigger" in his work at least until World War II, apparently regarding the term as no more offensive than "fuck" and "cunt." Compared to his published remarks about Jews, however, "nigger" seems almost offhand, and the boy who felt out of place in his old neighborhood grew up to write an early novel, *Moloch, or, This Gentile World*, in large part to ruminate on what was for him the insidious mystery of Jewishness.

The high school in the old neighborhood was probably no better academically than the one Schnellock and the others attended in Bushwick. Miller most keenly felt the lack of cultural context in the presentation of subject matter: facts and events were taught rather as if they were Platonic absolutes instead of living, interrelated aspects of the human story. Still, he had his own private curriculum, anchored in a complete set of the Harvard Classics his parents had given him, and he supplemented this with an enthusiastic engagement with the popular entertainments of his time and place: six-day bicycle races; wrestling and boxing matches; and the theater, especially burlesque, which he fell hard for with his first exposure to it around the age of fifteen.

Though the origins of the form lie in Old World folk performances and folk-based forms like commedia dell'arte that made fun of class distinctions, burlesque in America achieved unprecedented popularity, especially in New York in the last quarter of the nineteenth century. The reasons for this lie mainly in the character of the country, for burlesque as it evolved in America played to deeply ingrained predilections. It was crude and violent in its "dramaturgy." It shamelessly catered to the endemic bigotry of the national culture. It savagely mocked high art, particularly music and literature. It also made fun of all kinds of misfortune, from physical deformity to poverty. Finally and increasingly it was sexually suggestive—bawdy, intensely teasing, while stopping just short of being pornographic.

The Brooklyn boy loved it in all its tawdriness, its cruel humor, its prejudices, its sexuality. In the darkness of the hall and the focused lights of the stage, in the deliberate thinness of the make-believe, things otherwise off-limits were not simply allowed, they were celebrated. Here the masks were joyfully hurled aside and the knock-down power of a frontier-formed culture was in plain view. Here, Miller felt, were American realities, indeed deeply human ones, and it is possible that there never was for him another form of entertainment as satisfying on so many fronts. He learned to love high art and the culture of the Old World and the Orient. But burlesque wasn't art; it was life itself, in the raw, and this was what one day he would aspire to reproduce in his own writing.

In 1909 higher education was hardly the automatic next step for high school graduates, especially not for children of Henry Miller's socioeconomic class. After high school most such kids picked up a lunch pail or began punching a time clock. But because of his superior academic performance Miller seemed like a good candidate for college, and his German instructor recommended he try for a scholarship at Cornell. When he didn't get it he made a half-hearted try at the City College of New York but soon dropped out. By 1910 he was punching a clock, just like every boy he'd associated with in high school, commuting across the river to lower Manhattan where he was a file clerk for a cement company. Such a development might well have meant that the world would never hear the name Henry Miller. But Miller was cut from a different cloth, stubbornly unwilling to do what was then popularly referred to as "the world's work." So Miller, the failed Ivy Leaguer, the college dropout, the time-server working in literature's mortuary—filing dead records for a cement company—refused to submit to his cultural and personal fate. Instead, he embarked on a daring, audacious course, one that defied all the conventions of his background: he began a lifelong career as a sexual adventurer; and at the same time he determined that, despite what college faculties might think, he would continue his self-directed studies, reinventing himself as a man of culture, able to converse on a wide variety of subjects like his heroes, Spengler and Arthur Schopenhauer.

The World of Sex

The sexual adventures began in a manner then common enough: he became one of a group of young men who found courage in numbers when they paid their occasional visits to the numerous whorehouses in Manhattan's Herald Square area. His initiation into the mysterious world of sex thus came at a price—several actually. There was, of course, the entrance fee. And then there followed the almost inevitable doses of gonorrhea—though these were regarded as a badge of initiation into the secret order of full manhood and as such could be boasted about at the office, the bar, the sports arena. And then, the final, most lasting price: that conflicted attitude toward women and sex that was also contracted in the houses, a combina-

tion of assumed male superiority, crass usage, and genuine affection for the girls that had at its base a substantial
something of the son's worshipful regard for the mother
figure.

Quickly, he graduated to a more involved sexual relationship when he took up with a woman he met while
giving ham-handed piano lessons in Brooklyn for thirty-
five cents an hour. Pauline Chouteau, as she was then
calling herself, was old enough to have a grown son of her
own, but she found "Harry," as she called him, irresistibly
attractive, and as for Miller, he found the daily sex she
provided a marvelous antidote to his deadening job. Soon
enough, however, he grew alarmed at the frequency and
violence of their coupling: on the floor, in the bathtub, on
the piano stool—wherever the frenzy found them. This
was so constant that he began to keep a kind of calendar
of their carnality, checking off the days when he'd had sex.
But then, finding no blank spaces on it that would indicate abstinence, he abandoned the shameful record. Even
with her son in the next room where he lay dying of tuber-
culosis, Pauline herself was delighted to stay aboard this
sexual express. And if Miller had his private misgivings,
they weren't enough to cause him to get off, either, and so
when his parents gave him the tuition money to enter
Cornell, he took it to Pauline's—only a few blocks down

Decatur—and hid out there until he'd gone through it all, at which point he shamefacedly returned to his parents' house and confessed all. They already knew, his comings and goings at Pauline's having been reported by the neighbors.

The express rattled perilously on. Pauline became pregnant, and Miller, by now sated, watched this development at some unknowable remove, perhaps like that he'd earlier developed while witnessing the hopeless conflict between Louise and Lauretta. One evening when he returned home from work he found Pauline had aborted what he callously called the "seven-month toothache," the dead fetus enshrouded in a towel in a dresser drawer.

The event—whether natural or induced—appeared to have solved part of his predicament, how to rid himself of the Pauline problem. But not all of it. For that he would have to find somewhere to go, somewhere far beyond the suddenly too-tight confines of Brooklyn. So, he did what so many had before him: in 1913 he fled into the anonymity of the West, fetching up at the continent's end, California, where he found work as an agricultural laborer. The work was rough, and though he'd made himself into something of a physical culture nut back in Brooklyn, he wasn't prepared for stoop labor, and his hands were tender. The boys razzed him a bit about this, but as had happened years earlier when he'd been thrown into Bush-wick's boyhood briar patch, so here Miller made his way, not with his muscles but with his mouth. "Yorkie," as the boys called him, could talk. He was a tale spinner.

Talk

He'd always been able to do it, but never consistently.
There were often enough times when to his friends he
seemed a tongue-tied, timid stammerer, awed by some
stranger of supposedly greater learning or presence. But
then, suddenly, something voltaic would surge through
him and he would begin talking in torrents, long rushing
streams of images, anecdotes, narrative fragments, wildly
adventurous associations, startling and bizarre metaphors,
lies so outrageous they strangely compelled a kind of belief. So now, in the fruit orchards of San Pedro and Chula
Vista, working his generously proportioned mouth that
appeared to have been constructed precisely for this purpose, he could render his rough audience speechless, as
if he were an avatar of those folk monologists of another

era, assembling out of the brilliant air worlds unimaginable to his listeners. He did the work they did—though it is easy enough to imagine he was never the most industrious among them; he went with them to whorehouses on weekends; drank with them and laughed at the crude jokes they passed around. But in this singular sense he was a man apart. "When I wished to," he remembered,

> when I had the itch, I could single out any man, in any stratum of society, and make him listen to me. I could hold him spellbound, if I chose, but, like a magician, or a sorcerer, only as long as the spirit was in me. At bottom I sensed in others a distrust, an uneasiness, an antagonism, which, because it was instinctive, was irremediable.

Sooner or later, he continued, he was bound to say something that would carve out an instant chasm between the spellbinder and his audience:

> The turn of a phrase, the choice of an unfortunate adjective, the facility with which the words came to my lips, the allusions to subjects which were taboo— everything conspired to set me off as an outlaw, as an enemy of society.[12]

There were other spellbinders abroad in California and elsewhere in these last prewar days, famous ones who could draw huge crowds when the authorities allowed Emma Goldman, Big Bill Haywood, John Reed, Elizabeth Gurley Flynn, Carlo Tresca, and other radicals to appear. The phonograph was yet in its infancy, and the age of radio was just dawning. But public speaking was a highly developed art, and Miller was drawn to it, as much perhaps because of the sheer spectacle of the phenomenon as the speakers' specific messages. One weekend afternoon he and a fellow worker were on their way to a San Diego whorehouse when they happened to see a notice that Goldman would be speaking in the city that day. The two men changed their plans and went to hear her, something that Miller more than half a century later was still calling a life-altering event. It's a good story, combining as it does two anti-establishment bugaboos—sex-for-pay and red radicalism—and it does not matter that much if Miller actually heard Goldman on that occasion (he may not have), because the fact is that subsequently he read about her and read some of her writings. By the time he returned to Brooklyn in 1914 he was a convert to the trade unionism movement, to free love, and to philosophical anarchism and began attending mass rallies where these causes were championed.

What drew him to these and kindred causes was that they ran militantly against the American mainstream. The America Miller had come to know had forsaken its radical idealism, he believed, and had instead become enslaved to the sordid, soul-killing idea of Progress, Progress in every aspect of life, Progress at all costs. Everything, even the private relations between a man and a woman in the dark-ness of a bedroom or in the bushes of a public park, was subject to this one great end: *forward.* In the first days of the Great War only the so-called lunatic fringe in Amer-ica was asking probing questions about the human costs of this, the spiritual toll of this worship of a god who de-manded such extravagant sacrifices.

Perhaps for Miller these costs were the more real and appalling because of what was happening in his own house-hold, where he watched his father falling farther and far-ther behind in the rat race, neglecting his business, and retreating into a boozy sentimentalism, as if in his own way he too wished to rebel against what this New World required of a man. Louise, her son felt, was at the same time becoming more and more a slave driver, the in-house personification of the tyrannous spirit of the age. With the menial labor he'd done in California fresh in his mind he was increasingly drawn to the notion that there must be more to human existence than the brutish necessity of earning your bread by the sweat of your brow until at last you keeled over and croaked. And here even the radical politics of Goldman and Haywood didn't seem adequate to him for all its talk about the dignity of all work and the moral necessity of giving the workingman a fair shake. That wasn't enough for him. He didn't want a fair shake; he wanted something else altogether, though he couldn't yet call its name. Thus, while he considered himself a political radical (and always would), he was increasingly drawn to thinkers who suggested there was another plane of existence beyond politics, one that had little to do with political movements or Progress or personal economic advancement. Madame Helena Blavatsky for one, a cloudy yet compelling mystagogue whose studies in Oriental religions led her to posit the existence of a realm of being that had nothing to do with the moneygrubbing of the modern world. The Welsh writer and philosopher John Cowper Powys, a hawk-faced man who Miller thought was "all flame, all spirit," was another and even more significant influence—a powerhouse lecturer with an attachment to the natural world that was an antidote to the soullessness of the city and much else of modern living. Benjamin Fay Mills was another influence, a reformed Christian evangelist who had made something akin to Emerson's conversion eighty years earlier, from a strict orthodoxy to a more mystical worship in which Christ was only one of the gateways to salvation. Miller was enough taken with what he took to be Mills's message that he volunteered his services as an usher and alms collector at Mills's appearances in the New York area.

Meanwhile, the slaughterhouse of daily, meaningless drudgery loomed ever closer as Louise insisted with increasing urgency that he join his father at the tailor shop and so save the family from ruin. Only Henry, she wailed, now stood between the family and starvation.

Entering the Slaughterhouse

To Miller the tailor shop seemed somehow a particularly degrading form of work, as if he were being condemned to spend the rest of his days pressing out the farts the customers had left in their pants, as he so pungently put it. Nonetheless, he could see nothing else possible under the circumstances and knuckled under to his mother's demands. His father had new business forms made up, reading "Henry Miller & Son," which must have looked to that son like the official stamp and seal of his fate. No escape now, only the weary commute to the Bowery stop where he would get off so that at least he might get some exercise in the walk uptown. At that morning hour the place was filled with others on foot, some of them stumbling and shuffling—pimps and coke-heads, Miller said, "beggars, touts, gunmen, chinks, wops, drunken micks. All gaga for a bit of food and a place to flop." Miller himself possessed these necessities, of course, and a job to go to, but spiritually he felt as much on the streets as these men in the Bowery, homeless and alone.

The shop itself was no better. If anything, it might be worse than the streets, where at least there was a kind of freedom, even if it was only the freedom to starve. At the shop his immediate associates were the three Jewish men in the busheling room to whom he felt an instant aversion. But he couldn't be around them for very long without privately coming to realize that each of them had a fund of personal culture far richer than his own. They could talk about philosophy, music, and literature with an assurance he lacked, despite his frenzied, unsponsored reading. Yet here they were, wage slaves, as he saw it, working away in a back room to cut and shape cloth for men who in too many instances were not their intellectual equals. The longer he was forced to look down their road, the same one he was traveling, the bleaker it looked, the pavement each day harder, the steel-and-concrete canyons narrower, more inescapable, the "new world eating into me, expropriating me." Soon, he began imagining, he would be swallowed whole, just another nameless sacrifice.

Meanwhile, in the front room where his father greeted

such customers as there still were he saw how truly hope-less his true task here was—to save his father. Those re-maining customers were for the most part his father's cro-nies, drinking partners who paid—tardily, if ever—for the expertly tailored suits the Jewish cutters in back turned out. These were men who needed to keep up the appear-ances they could no longer afford, men who felt they must positively sparkle when they walked across the avenue to the Wolcott Hotel for their eleven o'clock drinks, and in Henry Miller, Senior, they had a man who understood this, for their needs were his own. They were all like Paul Dexter, a "ten-thousand-dollar-a-year-man," a brilliant monologist, but who was always temporarily between po-sitions and who frequently disappeared on week-long bats. Or else they had some tarnished Old World background like the penniless baron who had fallen on hard times in this New World where he had contracted syphilis like some conquistador out of the age of exploration. Some-where along the road they had all lost their way and now were reduced to trading as best they could on the appear-ances Henry Senior provided on credit. In their boozy bonhomie at the Wolcott bar and the other bars along Fifth Avenue they could forget for a few hours how lost they were. And sometimes they could extend that forget-fulness, that alcoholic anodyne, into the evening, because Miller's father might bring one or another of them home to Decatur Street, thrusting them into Louise's baleful presence. Only for a meal maybe, or an overnight stay, just until a temporary financial inconvenience had been straightened out. Once, so Miller claimed, his father even took one of these guests to bed with him. However that may have been, it is certainly believable that often enough Miller had to go to his own bed with the *Nachtmusik* of his mother raging at her sodden husband whose need for male friendship was hurtling his business toward a financial abyss.

While bearing passive witness to this process Miller began to court a pianist named Beatrice Wickens. Pauline was still in the picture but now very much in its background. Beatrice was about Miller's own age, whereas Pauline was considerably older, and besides, the younger woman had an active interest in the arts and could discuss with Miller some of the books he was tearing through— Spengler, Schopenhauer, Nietzsche, Freud, the Greek dramatists, Dostoyevsky, Gorky. For a brief time Miller saw both women, but Pauline clearly belonged to the past and Beatrice to the future.

One thing remained the same in the new relationship, and this was the frantic, acrobatic, improvisational nature of the couple's lovemaking, as if Miller required this form of aphrodisiac. But there was now as well a new quality and a complication, for Beatrice had had a very traditional

Catholic upbringing and carried within her a profound ambivalence about the pleasures of the body. The more fun she had in one of their torrid encounters, Miller claimed, the deeper her subsequent torment. Nothing could have been more calculated to excite Miller's anger and ferocious contempt, though at the time he might not have been able to say just why. But for a man who claimed his mother had so early instilled the spirit of rebellion in his heart, all his combative energies were strongly stirred by what he regarded as a pious and ultimately cankered denial of the body and its perfectly natural needs. So here, Beatrice's post-coital fits of remorse provoked Miller's most inventive cruelty. Still, they continued to have sex, Miller perhaps perversely spurred on to more incessant demands by the prospect of Beatrice's anguished tears. What else could they then do but marry? And this they unhappily did in 1917, and then quickly set to work building their respective redoubts, she the shrewish, humiliated wife, and he the feckless, henpecked husband. By the time their daughter Barbara was born in 1919, Miller was staying away from home as much as possible, and when he did venture back, often enough he had in tow one or another of his cronies, a reprise of the situation in his parents' household.

By then, though, Miller's father had drifted beyond even that sad state and was sleeping away ever larger stretches of his days in simple avoidance technique. Remembering this period, his son would eventually describe the old man snoring away in his Morris chair, "dead as a crater," or—in an even more invidious metaphor—"like a dodo which buries its head in the sand and whistles out of its asshole."[13] Clearly, his continuance at the tailor shop had become pointless, and Miller gladly quit for a bewildering succession of temporary jobs, all of which he speedily dropped, much to his wife's distress and mounting contempt. Nothing suited her Henry—nothing useful at any rate—because by now it had occurred to him that what he really wanted to do was to become a writer.

He had, however, absolutely no idea how this ambition could be realized. Already, he'd turned over half a library, reading through the works of the great. And in the tailor shop he had met an honest-to-god living, working writer, Frank Harris. Reading was fine in its way; certainly a writer must be well read. And Harris's colorful personality was attractive: it was grand indeed to be able to sail into a tailor shop to be fitted out for a yachting costume. Still, neither reading nor Harris's literary status showed the way into the actual, solitary act of composing. Maybe it was a matter of the right materials. So he bought pens and a notebook, but they were dead things in his hands. Then somehow he got a monstrous desk out of the tailor shop and into his Brooklyn flat where it squatted, square in the midst of the living room. Yet when he sat down to it with his proper materials nothing happened. He himself was as dead as a crater, sitting there, staring at the unforgiving blankness of the page. He refused to believe he had nothing to say because for some years now he had been composing in his head dialogue, scenes, character sketches, vignettes as he shuttled to and from his menial jobs. What then was the trick, the hidden spring, the magic formula that would release interior invention, turning thought or conversation into words written on a waiting page?

Manhattan Monologist

Maybe he'd been born in the wrong place—Brooklyn, USA—at the wrong time, this soulless modern age of Progress? He asked his old friend Emil this question many times on his visits to Schnellock's Fiftieth Street studio. He would come bounding up the stairs to the studio, filled with an electric vigor, clad in his studiously shabby army shirt and battered felt hat, brimming with new stories and observations gleaned from his voracious reading. But then, the question: was it merely his bad luck to be only an American instead of a European? Perhaps to find an answer by way of context, he would pump Emil for reminiscences of his time abroad, using Schnellock's mounted wall map of the Continent as a constant point of reference. But what really riveted him was a large map of Paris.

He studied that as if it were a kind of code he was meant to crack, tracing with his fingers the archaic meander of its streets, the grand arc the river made through the city's heart.

All of this of course was when it was just the two of them. In the company of others, men with some artistic or intellectual cachet, Miller would be mostly silent, almost mute. It infuriated his host because, better than anyone, Schnellock knew how Miller could talk when the fit was on him. Yet in the presence of these prestigious strangers his old friend seemed cowed, suddenly and quite literally just a Brooklyn boy. In more comfortable company it could be quite different. Then, maybe, something said—the expression of some bit of vanity, a piety, the mindless repetition of a reigning shibboleth—would set him off on verbal flights that transfixed and transformed his listeners with what Schnellock recalled as Miller's "magnificent life-giving words, words that seemed to restore to us what life had robbed us of. Truth, lies, fantasy, drama, invention"—and a sidesplitting humor so overwhelming it hurt. And there were a very few occasions when Miller could do this in the presence of those strangers he appeared to regard as his betters. On these occasions it was as if he'd suddenly said to himself, "Fuck everything," and then would "sweep away all barriers and take the company by storm," as Schnellock put it.

In the aftermath of such a performance Schnellock would find himself besieged with requests for Miller's address or phone number. How could they get hold of this guy? When was Emil going to invite him back, and couldn't they please be included? Yet if Schnellock did arrange such an occasion, Miller might well arrive wrapped in an impenetrable silence. After one of these aggravating non-performances and as Emil was berating him, Miller flew into a rage in the course of which and in an apparent reference to the brilliance of his talk and its very occasional nature, he uttered the warning words, *"That's totem and taboo!"* The proximate reference here, of course, would have been to Freud's controversial book on exogamy and other taboos of primitive cultures. But what could the retort have meant in this context? It might have meant simply that Miller wasn't a trained seal, a trick pony who could perform on demand. That would be consistent with his characteristic tendency to work always against the grain, whatever the grain was at a given time or situation. But maybe it meant something more as well. Maybe it meant that Miller himself didn't really know where the improvised flights came from and wasn't able to summon them at will. Maybe he was both baffled and troubled, too, by the very unpredictability of this talent. Was it even a talent, or was it instead the recrudescence of that broad strand of craziness in his family line, the taboo of his

tribe? If it was this, no wonder a conversational consider-
ation of it was off limits, both for himself and for his closest friend.

At some point, however, when Miller had spoken to
Schnellock again of his helpless thrashings in the literary
wilderness—he wanted after all to be a *writer* not some
mere street-corner sorcerer—Schnellock told him that the
way out for him was to write the same way he talked, an
easy enough observation perhaps. But in truth there yawns
always a chasmic divide between the lightning quickness
of speech and the more meditative act of writing, and few
writers can easily bridge it, though many have tried and
precisely because the former feels closer to whatever the
original inspiration was.[14]

Cosmodemonic

While Miller continued his inevitably amateurish literary
gropings, tensions in the household continued to inten-
sify. The huge desk plumped down in the middle of the
living room was a constant affront to Beatrice, who saw
it as a symbol of Miller's childish impracticality and his
multiple failures as husband, father, and provider. In this
context the fact that he was also proving a bust as a writer
was almost beside the point. Early in 1920, though, matters changed when he talked his way into a well-paying
job as an employment manager at Western Union.

Beatrice could hardly believe it, and Miller could hardly
believe it, either, once he understood what the job involved: the heartless, systematic exploitation of the half-
crazed starvelings the company employed to deliver its

telegrams. Like the three cultured Jews in the tailor shop's busheling room, many of the aspirants who appeared before Miller, cap in hand, seemed to him men of some breeding and intelligence. Yet all were now merely meat for the "slaughterhouse" that was modern American capitalism.

At first, he claimed (doubtless with a subsequently applied comic exaggeration) that he accepted every last condition of his employment, asking no questions of his superiors. If on a given morning he received a directive that no cripples be hired, he turned away all cripples. If on another day the word came down that all messengers over forty-five were to be fired without notice, he fired them. No more Jews, then no more Jews. But then on the casual remark of a superior something within him snapped. The man had mused aloud that someone ought to write a book about how the company (which Miller styled the "Cosmodemonic Telephone Company") was providing the necessary breeding ground for a whole new generation of Horatio Algers. To Miller, who saw daily what those breeding grounds actually were, and who had to understand just what it was that he, Henry Miller, was himself involved in, the remark was as cruel as it was stupid. Later, in *Tropic of Capricorn*, he remembered of this moment that what he wanted most to do in life was to utterly destroy the secular myth of Horatio Alger with a book of a very different sort, one that would reveal the Horatio Alger story as the "dream of a sick America." There follows a passage that might well have been reminiscent of those sudden and perhaps even unbidden outbursts that so mesmerized the men at Emil Schnellock's studio, as Miller imagines his anti-Alger figure

> mounting higher and higher, first messenger, then operator, then manager, then chief, then superintendent, then vice-president, then president, then trust magnate, then beer baron, then Lord of all the Americas, the money god, the god of gods, the clay of clay, nullity on high, zero with ninety-seven thousand decimals fore and aft.

He had a vacation coming to him, two weeks. He took three, writing an astonishing five thousand or more words a day at Schnellock's studio until he was finished. He called the book *Clipped Wings*, and from his later references to it and from its few surviving scraps it's possible the best thing about it may have been its title, a mordant turn on Western Union's winged logo. Miller's characters are twelve messengers, all of them deformed angels whose wings have been clipped by the corporation's exploitation of them. Possibly he had in mind a group portrait such as Edgar Lee Masters had done in *Spoon River Anthology* and Sherwood Anderson in *Winesburg, Ohio*. But everyone

Miller showed the manuscript to disparaged it, some evidently telling him it was so dreadful he should never again think of writing. Many years later, both in print and in filmed interviews, Miller said he himself finally understood just how bad a book it was. Its saving grace, he said, was that the writing of it taught him what it was to fail at something genuinely worth failing at—being an author. This was 1922.

She

Within a year of that creative failure it was obvious that
Miller had suffered a domestic one as well: his marriage
was irretrievably wrecked. It had never been a harmonious
one, and the arrival of the baby hadn't improved matters.
By now Beatrice was both deeply wounded by his brutal
treatment of her and contemptuous of his literary striv-
ings. As for Miller, he no longer made any effort to con-
ceal his flagrant philandering and was rarely at home.

One summer's night, on the prowl around Times Square
and with money in his pocket, he wandered into a taxi-
dance hall, danced with one of the girls, and felt his life
forever changed. It was.

For that night at least, the dancer was using the name
June Mansfield, but like so many in the New World to

which she had come from the Old, she had many others, and despite what speedily developed into an obsessional interest in every least detail of her being, Miller never learned all the ones she had sailed under. Nor was he ever able to penetrate the layered mysteries of her character and her past. He was to spend the following decade trying to decipher her, as if he were some rakish, feverish Champollion to her Rosetta stone—whether she was whore, or angel, or the angel of death. At various moments she was any one of these to him and perhaps all of them at once. In the beginning she was a dark goddess. At the end, he was calling her a "Jewish cunt." But first and last she was his muse, the personification of that mythic being—beautiful, all-powerful, changeful—who the male artist cannot choose but who instead merely nods in his direction and so inspires the best work that is in him. For Miller, June in one way and another inspired his three finest works, the *Tropics* and *Black Spring*. At the other end of his long career he was still trying to work out for himself what she meant to him, retelling the old stories through the endless pages of *The Rosy Crucifixion*, which Norman Mailer was right about when he called it a giant layer cake that fails to rise.

In the presence of her unearthly beauty, her powerful sexuality, he recognized instantaneously that here was the muse he'd read about in classical literature but never expected to meet. And he felt at the same time that she'd given him that nod that was both permission (to continue on with his lonely artistic quest) and invitation (to do so under her aegis). She told him she believed in his star, maybe more deeply than he himself did in the moment of their meeting. Later on, as their relationship lengthened and he began to sense that with her he was in far beyond his depth, he began to turn her from the muse of myth into a legend—which is more comprehensible because more narrative—so that he could write about her in the context of their lives together, where they went, how they lived. At last, when everything personally significant about the relationship had rotted away through infinite deceptions and betrayals, savage fights, transatlantic estrangements, and June's descent into madness, she became what perhaps she was always meant to be for him: a darkly glowing metaphor of America, in the somber light of which he composed the finest things he had in him. All of which—the wild contradictions, the changes, the sublime heights and abysmal depths—may suggest—*may*—why Miller hung onto June for so long, through bewilderment and poverty, through degradation, and the most awful humiliation a man might suffer.

What he might actually have felt in that moment of meeting cannot, of course, be known. He made several attempts to recapture that in words, none better than in *Capricorn* where he describes June moving toward him through the murk and sleaze of the taxi-dance hall. And what makes this particular effort special is that it is at once both powerful in its language and hopeless in its emotional aspirations, because this isn't a human who is being described. It is some other order of being to whom (or should it be to "which"?) none of the known rules apply: She, for whom everything must be undergone.

She seemed to him at first blue-black in color, but the longer he stared and the closer she came, he saw that she was an ageless chalk-white. And she wasn't moving toward him, or even gliding, which would be the expectable verb here:

> There was not just the flow to and from, but the endless chute, the voluptuousness of intrinsic restlessness. She was mercurial and at the same time of a savory weight. She had the marmoreal stare of a faun embedded in lava.
>
> . . .
>
> The earth slid rapidly beneath my bewildered feet. I moved again out of the earth belt and behold, my hands were full of meteoric flowers. I reached for her with two flaming hands but she was more elusive than sand. I thought of my favorite nightmares, but she was unlike anything which had made me sweat and gibber. In my delirium I began to prance and neigh.

I bought frogs and mated them with toads. I thought of the easiest thing to do, which is to die, but I did nothing. I stood still and began to petrify at the extremities. That was so wonderful, so healing, so eminently sensible, that I began to laugh way down inside the viscera like a hyena crazed with rut. Maybe I would turn into a rosetta stone!

Whatever else this passage means—and it is dense with meanings; whoever June Mansfield Smerth Smith was—and she was doubtless many things except the vile name Miller used when he was trying to rid himself of her haunting presence—these words, written years after the fact, tell us that when Miller saw the nameless woman moving toward him, when he first held her body in his arms, he felt himself hurled into some dimensionless state where all things were possible, especially the possibility that he had after all authentic artistic greatness within. But in order to realize that particular possibility he would have to catch hold of this being and hang on through all her protean shifts and states. This is the only way to make sense of what he willingly underwent over the next seven years.

He was ever the comic exaggerator, and there is no single subject on which he is more unreliable than June. But there can be no doubt that meeting her was in truth a life-altering experience for him, and that by the time they had finally parted ways he felt his soul had been keel-hauled. But finally and most importantly, the very torments he suffered over her were magically transformed into the instruments of salvation, which is one definition of art.

The Henry Miller who had walked into the taxi-dance hall in the summer of 1923 was a husband, a father, and a man with a responsible job. A little more than a year later almost everything had changed. He had divorced Beatrice and married June; his contact with little Barbara was sporadic at best and would gradually become almost non-existent; he had quit Western Union; and he and June were living in a Brooklyn flat they could in no way afford while bills piled up around their feet like snowdrifts. Most significantly, he had embarked on a quest to become a writer. This last was also to become a great problem, because though he now thought of himself as an artist, and though he had somehow acquired his muse, he had by 1924 entered a period of almost five years of drift, apathy, and indecision in which there was an enormous amount of talk about writing but little to show for it, only two botched novels, unpublished in his lifetime and which would never have been published had he not become famous in the 1960s. Through all this June clung to her primeval belief that "Val," as she called him, possessed the stuff of greatness somewhere within him, though it is clear that at various points that belief seriously flickered. An illusionist herself, she seems to have at least half-believed that writing was an act of sortilege, and perhaps Miller himself may have wanted to believe this as well, though his experience of hammering out the manuscript about the twelve deformed angels ought to have told him something different. And maybe it was this shared illusion that kept them together through evictions, unpaid and unpayable debts, get-rich-quick-without-working schemes, the endless lies they told to creditors, friends, and each other; and the increasing chaos and clutter of their daily lives. All this could make sense if in fact Val was really on the path to greatness instead of being what many must have thought—a bum and a windbag. So, while he and his cronies spent days in endless talk, joking and drinking and walking the streets, June held down one job and another. From time to time the would-be writer actually did bestir himself, making solitary excursions in the greater New York area, looking for potential literary material. But there was no method to these, and because he was so largely self-educated and so insatiably curious he was easily sidetracked into intellectual labyrinths where he would lose himself for weeks at a time, reading up on, for instance, the history of chicle harvesting for a story he planned to write on chewing gum. Without his intending it, however, Miller's wanderings and investigations of everything from amusement parks to professional wrestling were providing him with a deep knowledge of American culture that would stand him in creative stead in the future. Now, however, that was not apparent to either Miller or June, and as the months rolled on June began to wonder whether she had misjudged her Val, that he was all talk and little substance.

Perhaps simply to make ends meet she began to "gold-dig"—a thin euphemism for whoring—bringing home to Val cash from her various "admirers." She evidently had extensive experience in this line of work by the time she and Miller met, and so in their increasingly exiguous circumstances it might have been natural enough for her to resort to it once again. He tried not to imagine what she had to do to get the money she brought him, but with a mind like his he could hardly have escaped knowing what was really going on. At one point, for instance, the Millers ran a speakeasy that had a bedroom attached, and while Miller and his pals sat in the kitchen spinning tales and drinking, June took favored customers back to the bedroom.

Still, it was a day-to-day kind of existence the couple lived, and this began to cut ever more deeply into the relationship. By the end of 1925 matters had become desperate enough for them to separate. And so at the age of thirty-four Miller moved back to the parental home on Decatur where he would sit in the parlor for hours with his typewriter, sometimes pecking at the machine, but mostly staring out the window, wondering why the magic stream wouldn't flow for him. When guests were to visit he would hastily pack up his typewriter and papers and hide in a closet until they left. His mother was ashamed: maybe Henry was just another family nutcase.

The following year the couple reunited, but things weren't any better. Miller was still blocked, and June, now exasperated with the man who had begun referring to himself as "The Failure," was openly selling herself around in the Village. In the fall the nadir they'd reached at the end of the previous year was revealed to have been a false bottom when June began a lesbian relationship with a mentally disturbed artist named Jean Kronski. Soon Jean and her grotesque puppet/companion, "Count Bruga," were living with the Millers, and soon after that June and Jean were sleeping together while The Failure consoled himself as best he could in the next bed. The women began openly talking of going to Europe together, making plans as if Miller wasn't there, and one day when he returned from an outing he found them gone, leaving a note behind saying only that they had shipped for Paris. In mingled rage and despair he broke every piece of furniture in the place, howling so wildly that the landlady feared for his life and came down to try to comfort him.

Months later, June returned, mercifully minus Jean, yet still carrying a considerably travel-battered Count Bruga. And so once more the sorry dance began again, with Miller now but one among several men vying for June's attentions in an eerie reprise of that initial encounter when she was a taxi-dancer. His main rival appeared to be a man who wrote jokes for the *New Yorker* cartoonist Peter Arno. Roland Freedman was an older man whom June called Pop and who was in his own way as smitten with her as Miller had been—and in many ways still was—though he seems never to have thought of her as a mythological being. June herself, if she was not a goddess, was at least remarkably resourceful and now devised a new scheme to shake more gold out of Pop. Representing herself as an aspiring novelist who lacked only money so that she could quit her degrading work for literature, she got Freedman to put her on a kind of retainer while she wrote the novel she had for so long had in mind. The actual work, of course, would have to be secretly done by Miller, and it is a gauge of how desperate and dangerous his attachment to June had become that he agreed to serve as her galley slave, and that after so long a period when he could write almost nothing, now, in this new humiliating situation, he was able to crank out page on page of a manuscript he called *Moloch, or, This Gentile World*. Freedman must have been smitten indeed to have admired the thing enough to give June the money to go to Europe for several months in late summer 1928. Her husband joined her, a kind of stowaway.

The novel was in fact dreadful, a lurching, unconvincing hodgepodge of invective, random musings, and bigotry about a character who hates almost everything, most especially his immediate surroundings, the grimy city and its even more grimy inhabitants. Blacks, Chinese, American Indians, East Indians, epileptics—all are casually, even joyously slandered. But as the title suggests, it is the Jews who come in for the worst of it. Here there is neither casualness nor joy, only a species of venom the world would soon come to know too well. All this is delivered from a wavering, uncertain point of view and in language that at times is stupefyingly stilted: "Like a butterfly in the palpitant tomb of its chrysalis, Marcelle fluttered and yearned with nubile wings for the miracle of the advent of dawn. In the surrender of a caress she looked for the swoon which would bring about her deliverance." And so on.

Just about the only thing in these pages that retrospectively would suggest the Henry Miller of only three years later is the cruelty of the humor, a bequest to him from American culture's bedrock. If *Clipped Wings* was, as he later claimed, bad enough to stiffen his backbone and put sulphur in his blood, *Moloch* by such logic should have made him feel as if he were sitting on top of the world. It was another very bad book, to be sure, as maybe even he would then have known. But, after all, he had now written an actual, full-length novel under unimaginable pressure. And the payoff was a trip to the legendary Old World, a trip that would take him and his wife far away from her faceless and unnumbered admirers. The fact that June was supposed to have written it and that the money the Millers would use to visit France, Belgium, and eastern Europe had come from a man who was bedding her might not have seemed in that moment of much importance to a man living almost completely within a garish illusion that was beginning to take on distinct aspects of a nightmare.

Not much is known about the European escape. For a man who'd been dreaming of just such an opportunity for years—tracing Paris's streets with his dreaming fingers and devouring heaping helpings of Europe's writers and thinkers—Miller was oddly silent about it once they had come back to Brooklyn, mostly complaining to friends about the hygienic hardships an American faced over there where an indoor toilet seemed something of a novelty. This sounds a bit like the ultra-fastidious *Innocents Abroad*—published sixty years earlier by a man who wore white suits to visually separate himself from the world's nastiness.

The couple found a flat on Brooklyn's Clinton Street and settled again into what appeared to be the old routine, with June going back to a restaurant where she'd worked before while Miller stayed home to write another novel. Actually, though, there were differences, and what the Millers now began to enact was a dark reconfiguration of a fairy tale in which Beauty goes out to service her bestial customers while the Unpromising Hero is condemned to a tower cell until he can spin the chaff of their life into a story that rescues Beauty from her sexual servitude. This wasn't, however, the way the tale ultimately turned out. June went back to the Pepper Pot as before, and as before she went to bed with certain of her customers, particularly an insurance man with money to spend on her. Pop, too, was in the picture but not so centrally. By this time June's drug use, which before had been casual, was deepening toward true dependency, and her behavior, always dramatic and eccentric, had become occasionally very erratic. At the same time, her attitude toward Val's writing had narrowed to a narcissistic obsession: he must write a novel about her and thus ensure her immortality. Nothing short of this would make her sacrifices worthwhile.

This, she apparently felt, was the great book Miller had in him, that vital spark she had intuited the first night in the dance hall. *Moloch* had served its purpose, but it was after all an apprentice work.

Miller probably had learned a few valuable lessons in writing it. He'd learned that bigotry, while it was simple enough to express, wasn't sufficient to sustain an extended work of fiction. You had to have something else going on to engage readers over hundreds of pages. Fiction, at least as he understood it then, was not finally argument. It was story. And what was the story he had to tell if not that of June, this endlessly mysterious, darkly compelling creature who had put him through so much? Actually, something akin to this had already occurred to him a few years back when June had deserted him for Jean and Paris. One day as he sat brooding on this humiliating injustice, he'd begun to type, furiously, feverishly, and before the impulse had spent itself he'd turned out some thirty single-spaced pages about her.

So with June out hustling at the Pepper Pot, Miller turned back to these notes. But in the same way he had been inspired to write *Clipped Wings* to demolish the Alger story, now in the manuscript he was calling *Lovely Lesbians* he began not to immortalize June but instead to ruthlessly expose her layers of lies, her cruel treatment of him. The characters of June (Hildred) and Jean (Vanya) are thus depicted as the enemies of the gelded husband, Tony Bring, callously neglecting him and even psychologically torturing him with their mutual obsession and their bizarre ambition to create a gang of puppets like Count Bruga. Even their occasional concern for poor Tony is negatively portrayed, as when Hildred and Vanya together minister to his hemorrhoids. Daily, Miller writes, "they turned him over on his stomach and doctored his rectum. Between times they lubricated his system so thoroughly and conscientiously that if he had been a Linotype machine or a Diesel engine he would have functioned smoothly for a year to come." Then the women turn back to each other with their incessant chatter and equally incessant hammering as they whack the puppets into shape. This was hardly what June could have had in mind for her literary monument. Even the title, *Lovely Lesbians*, was bound to offend her because it caricatured a relationship that to her at least had been vitally important and filled with nuances that Miller grimly ignored in favor of cheap comedy and self-pity.

There is indeed still too much undigested self-pity in these pages and still too much generalized malice of the sort that makes *Moloch* such hard reading. Yet there are a few sentences here and there and one or two passages where the writer is able to let it rip, where a combustible combination of anger, grief, and despair allows him access to reaches of his imagination not available to him in *Moloch*. These are the places where the writer begins to learn how to say—and to *mean*—"Fuck everything!" Begins to learn how to say it at length and in words no less scabrous but which are stylistically richer.

And there is a passage near the manuscript's end that contains one of the keys that eventually would unlock the door that had thus far barred Miller from access to the full range and reach of his talent. In it the broken Tony Bring, whose body is "but a collection of bruises," thinks to himself that if only he had the necessary solitude and silence, he could reconstruct in exquisite detail every single thing that had ever happened to him, from birth to the present moment. But he doesn't have either solitude or silence. Instead he has only the hammering and the jawing of the lovely lesbians, busily and brazenly planning their desertion of him for Gay Paree. He will fix them yet, Bring thinks to himself. He will write about them and everything else as well. Writing well and fully will be the ultimate revenge. But not here, not in these pages, where it looks very much as if Miller had exhausted his creative energies, ending the novel with the image, at once bleak and destructive, of all his characters going down in a storm at sea, like the rotten vessels they were.

Exile

June couldn't have been happy about the manuscript in whatever version she saw it. But it is possible that her narcissism combined with her drug use to keep her in some sort of touch with her conviction that Val could yet write the great book about her even if *Lovely Lesbians* wasn't it. In any case, she was straight in her mind about one thing: Val had to go. She couldn't operate with him around the apartment all day. (She might have wanted to use it for business purposes.) And she might also have thought that Miller really could profit by a radical change of scenery that might spark off renewed creativity, whereas here he had sunk into an apathy that kept him in bed much of the day. Having finished his novel and sunk all his characters to the bottom of the sea, he seemed to have lost interest in almost everything except trying to keep tabs on her. The situation was intolerable.

In the same way she and Jean had begun a conversational promotion of their own escape to Paris in '27, now in late 1929 she began to promote Europe to Val, talking up Paris and Madrid as creative hot spots. In comparison, New York seemed sterile and gloomy, especially lately: there had been an ominous crash on Wall Street in October, and though things had stabilized somewhat, the country seemed to have gotten a bad case of the jitters. Her question wasn't so much Why not go to Europe? as it was Why would you stay here? June promised him she could get the money together for passage, and then, somehow, she would periodically wire him funds to keep him going. Soon enough, she would join him, and life would become authentic in a way it couldn't be here. It was a hard sell, for Miller was immobilized by June's web of intrigue—Old World, New World, what the hell difference did it make? When June thrust his steamship ticket on him one day in early 1930 he accepted it much as his beaten Tony Bring might have. And when she further informed him that for unspecified reasons it wouldn't be convenient for him to spend his last night at home he didn't put up a fight, only submissively trudged off down the street with his heavy luggage.

He spent that night walking from one place to another

on the East Side, then made his way to Emil Schnellock's studio in the morning for comfort, for courage, and for the ten bucks his old pal had on hand to see him across the sea. Schnellock went with him down to the docks and saw him aboard the ship in falling snow. From the deck Miller watched America sliding away from him, the world he had once loved, then learned to loathe. To him this was the old world, the known, in all its contradictions, its vulgarity, its untamed landscape, its mindless devotion to what he would call the money god. Ahead, ironically, was a new world about which he knew almost nothing except the high-flown words of its philosophers and writers. While the ship "blindly plunged like fate into the lone Atlantic" (as Melville had written of the "Pequod" in *Moby-Dick*) the lone man went below to his bunk and wept.

Part Two

Where the Writers Went

He was thirty-eight and must have felt twice that, dragging the heavy baggage of his past to a shabby hotel on the Left Bank: the suits the Jewish tailors had cut in his father's shop; his copy of *Leaves of Grass* by another Brooklyn guy who'd gotten a late start; and the manuscripts of his two unpublished novels which he couldn't bear to leave behind but which he must have known made poor bona fides for his literary pretensions.

No one in the great city was expecting him. He'd met a few people there back in '28 with June, but really he hadn't a single friend, and, trapped within his primitive French, his chances of making any were slim. He had no papers that would permit him to apply for even the most menial work, and he was here for quite another purpose than to land an odd job like so many of those he'd had in America. In any case, from the perspective of a French employer, a look at his résumé would hardly have proved impressive. True, in America a man might have to play many roles on his way up, but Miller's sole distinction was that he had failed in every one of his. He was, in short, essentially unemployable. If he was very careful he had just enough money to get by for a short time, but he was completely dependent on a wife who had all but booted him out the door of their apartment into the city's wintry streets. If she failed to wire funds to the American Express office for him, he would have to panhandle, steal, or starve.

What then could the lone man do to stave off a paralyzing onslaught of the blues but get out of his room and into the streets with notebook and pen, walking great distances and making notes on virtually anything he happened to see, from the life of the cafés to the carcasses of the newly slaughtered horses hanging from the market stall hooks at Les Halles? With these for subject matter, he could at least reach back across the waters to that world he'd left behind, incorporating his observations in long letters, most of them to Emil Schnellock.

There was a barely suppressed quality of desperation to these letters, evident not only in their torrential lengths and their reiterative suggestion that Emil drop everything to join Miller in Paris; but also in their random piling up of impressions and ruminations, as if Miller was really writing to save his soul. As for poor Emil, he could hardly have been equal to the task of being a faithful pen pal— as he was later to observe in a published reminiscence of this time. No one could have. And if his friend had so radically changed his own life, Schnellock had no similar reasons to do likewise: the successful stay at home, as Crèvecoeur had so long ago observed of the phenomenon of expatriation.

Miller was also writing to June but rarely received more in return than the occasional terse cable, ordering him to hold on, telling him that more money was on the way. She did manage to send him some occasionally, though not enough to keep him from descending steadily through the layers of the city's populace, moving to ever cheaper hotels, skipping more and more meals, cadging a drink from a friendly stranger, selling his well-cut suits for a fraction of their worth. At the same time back home, the Depression was tightening its hold almost weekly, and June's line of work was inherently boom-or-bust under the best of circumstances. The entire situation, Miller wrote Emil's brother Ned, was as depressing as it was baffling. For one thing, he hadn't imagined how crippling in a daily way his language deficiency would prove, how it would compound his solitude. But the solitude might not have been quite so crushing for this garrulous man had it not been that within it he could almost hear the sound of his literary failure. The manuscripts mocked him every time he had to pack them up and then unpack them in another of his forced removes; or when carrying some pages to a café where his hand would pause in puzzlement over this passage or that, wondering what the hell was wrong here.

"Why does nobody want what I write?" he asked Ned. "Jesus, when I think of being 38, and poor, and unknown, I get furious. I refuse to live this way forever. There must be a way out." But in an ironic way, his presence here in this unknown world seemed to have made that escape even more difficult to find, not less so. At least home, however hateful, had its familiar sights and sounds. Here there weren't even the old hatreds to orient him, and so in addition to having been rendered speechless and friendless, he had no emotional compass—except his feet, driven here and there by fear.

It didn't help that on the surface at least Paris still looked like Gay Paree. It was true that the Roaring Twenties with their throngs of American tourists and expatriate artists were phenomena of the past. But to a passerby, outside in the darkened street, the cafés still looked as crowded and brilliantly lit as ever. Theaters and concert halls were packed. At her exacting copy of an eighteenth-century palazzo in the Sixteenth Arrondissement, the Vicomtesse Marie-Laure de Noailles hosted her salons for the well-born and the talented. And as spring came on, lifting clouds and spirits, the grand boulevards began to fill up with *flaneurs*—those artful strollers whose purpose was to appear bound for nowhere in particular. France, and Paris especially, had apparently handsomely recovered from the Great War.

Beneath the flossy surfaces, though, the nation was in perilous shape and had not recovered from a war that had largely been fought on French soil. The nation's infrastructure had been devastated, with railroads, shipping facilities, and more than forty thousand miles of roads badly damaged or destroyed. Eight hundred thousand buildings had been destroyed and razed to the ground. Some of this destruction had been repaired in the years since the armistice, but by no means all of it, and the funds that were to have gone to this gigantic task as reparations from Germany had never amounted to more than a trickle. Within a year of Miller's arrival Germany's payments would be permanently suspended.

In New York and other American cities bread lines and soup kitchens were just becoming features of the national landscape. These weren't evident in Paris in 1930, but this was mostly because so many of the working men who might have thronged to them were dead or permanently disabled: France had suffered about a million-and-a-half fatalities in the war and another 740,000 severely wounded. Here was a deeper damage to the infrastructure than bridges and rail lines, because it would take a generation and more to repair.

Very little of this could have been grasped by the newly arrived American for whom the Great War had been at most a great abstraction, a faraway something he wished only to avoid. But the longer he stayed in France, the more the war's deep-set spiritual consequences became important to him, and eventually they would become literary dynamite like those tons of unexploded ordnance that lay just below the topsoil of the French landscape.

But here, at the very outset of his explorations, he just walked, took his random notes, wrote his torrential letters home, and scratched at his manuscripts. He poked into alleys and *impasses* and under the river's many bridges. He prowled the quarters of the permanently poor—the Eighteenth, Nineteenth, and Twentieth Arrondissements. He went to Les Halles at dawn to watch the work of the strongmen—*Les Forts*—hauling great carcasses on their shoulders. Also, the work of the hookers who hung out in the bars and cafés that ringed Victor Baltard's vast steel-and-glass marketplace.

When he took a table with his manuscripts at one of the old hangouts of the expatriates—the Dôme, for instance, or Hemingway's local, La Closerie des Lilas—he was being a bit of a poseur, and part of him knew that. Yet there was something else going on there as he sat, carefully nursing a coffee or a glass of wine, something he may not have known about himself, but which was proof against his many poses, his masks and disguises, his evasions and indecisions and prevarications. And this was a tough, knotty core of artistic integrity that made him show up for work before he even understood what the "work" was—way back there in Brooklyn when he had answered an obscure prompting and hauled his antediluvian desk from the tailor shop to his apartment, if only to sit at it in a kind of pre-artistic paralysis, wondering how it was that the dross of life could be transmogrified into imperishable passages of literature. It was this same core of integrity that was to save him in Paris, that kept him roving the city, taking his notes, and writing those letters bristling with arcana, autobiographical excursions, great slabs hacked out of books he found intriguing, as if he himself were an epistolary version of one of Les Forts, toting his raw learning, his needs and aspirations, on his back. It was this that saved him from surrendering to despair. And it was what saved him as well from becoming just another of those dreary dregs of the old expat scene, the ones you saw on the terrace of Le Dôme or the Lilas, talking endlessly, hopelessly of the great novel they were going to write, the great picture they were going to paint. Waverly

Root, an expat himself who wrote for the Paris edition of Colonel Robert McCormick's *Chicago Tribune*, passed by these types on his way to work at the outset of the 1930s. They were always going to do great things, he said, just as soon as they finished their beer. "Unfortunately," Root observed dryly, "the beer never ran out."[15] This was not to be Henry Miller's fate, any more than it was to become just another worn cog in the American economic meat grinder.

Later, after he'd broken into a clearing out of that wilderness the Old World had been for him, he would look back down the path he'd cut and find a dark, cautionary moral in the life and early death of Arthur Rimbaud, one of his prime literary heroes. Rimbaud's "vile fate," Miller wrote in *The Time of the Assassins*, had been to fatally mistake a pose for authenticity. He had been stunningly innovative while he was a *literary* outlaw, Miller said, but had become incurably false to himself when he adopted and lived out the pose of an actual outlaw, a common gunrunner. The lesson for Miller was both simple and stark: never mistake any pose you may choose to adopt at a given moment for the real thing, the actual work, the solitary encounter with your material, however humble. *Never* give up your art, not for anything. Sitting at a window table with his manuscript piled in front of him at La Closerie des Lilas and looking across to the Bal Bullier, Miller might well have been unable to articulate any of this. Nevertheless, it was there, deep within him. It was what kept him, however obscurely, lugging his hopeless manuscripts here and there about the city of his old dreams.

It was what prompted him one day to do something that on its surface seemed escapist but was not: he went to the movies. The choice of film provides a clue to the deeper motivation: it was the Luis Buñuel–Salvador Dalí collaboration *Un Chien Andalou.* What he'd heard about the film in advance is not known, but he must have known at least that it was modernist in some way, and so his decision to attend a showing of it must be seen as an effort to make some sort of contact with the current artistic life of the city, even if it was only to sit in a darkened room watching apparently disconnected images flit across a screen. What he made of the film at the time is likewise unknowable. When he wrote Emil about it, he said he didn't know what to make of it, "except subconsciously." But since the film made such a lasting impact on him, we might guess that he was intrigued by its formlessness, its sudden, jolting scenes of cruelty, which felt as if the artists were mysteriously *inflicting* these on audiences conditioned to regard movies as a passive form of entertainment. Subsequently, he made efforts at contacting Buñuel, Jean Cocteau (who had written an essay on the film), and the novelist Maurice Dekobra. He wrote these men letters—

doubtless in English—and though he got no replies, he told Emil they were nonetheless good letters, especially the one to Buñuel, which he claimed was even crazier than *Chien* itself. At the same time his ramblings about the city began to take on a new purpose as he hunted for bookshops, galleries, and exhibition spaces where the work of avant-garde artists was publicly available.

These first, blunt-edged efforts in this direction amount to an acknowledgment that since he had evidently failed as a writer in the conventional mode, he might as well explore unconventional possibilities. Here personal history and national character intersected with a strong cultural trend in western Europe. Miller's nature was rebellious from childhood—whether this was really his mother's fault or not. He had stubbornly sought his own way intellectually while still a schoolboy; had been drawn to radical politics and the occult as a young man; and he had behind him a highly unconventional history of sexual adventures. Who then could have been more disposed to the artistically unconventional, the radical, the determinedly offbeat than this American outcast? For America's soul at its center, so Miller believed, was originally all of these. Rebellious at the core, ungovernable, lawless, and given to odd passions, America was truest to itself when it listened to the inmost promptings of these impulses.

The Avant-Garde

True, he could not yet bring himself to ditch *Moloch* or the manuscript he was now calling *Crazy Cock*, and in fact he continued to slash and hack intermittently at the latter for more than a year before finally admitting to himself that it was the "vilest crap that ever was." But in *Un Chien Andalou* he had both literally and figuratively seen something new, and in his subsequent investigations of Dada and its militant successor, Surrealism, he discovered that here in France there existed artists who had rebelled against all received esthetic conventions to create works that were vital, daring, and unsettling.

The French avant-garde had in fact survived the war in ways many other aspects of the culture had not. By 1930 the avant-garde was arguably more influential than it had ever been, and at the glittering salons in her palazzo the Vicomtesse de Noailles not only entertained the city's *gratin* but also played the enthusiastic hostess to Buñuel, Dalí, Cocteau, Pablo Picasso, Georges Braque, and Henri Matisse. Also to Joan Miró.

It was Miró, the renegade Spaniard, who had most boldly articulated the anti-art impulse that united the avant-garde across all mediums and national boundaries. He wanted, he declared, to "assassinate painting." This was in 1927, by which point he was an accomplished artist much admired by his colleagues for the way he put paint on the canvas. But painting, he felt—all painting, including that of the modernists—had become soiled, corrupted by its chummy relationships with bourgeois society. It was time, therefore, to strike out into uncharted territory, creating paintings, drawings, collages that were so daring, so aggressively unconventional that they were bound to look hideous to the eye: raw, apparently haphazard, heedless of any recognized esthetics, and owing absolutely nothing to yesterday. In 1928 Miró exhibited his daring new work in Paris and successfully so. But he was hardly cheered by this. Writing to a friend, he said, "Right from the beginning of the exhibition I understood the danger of success and felt that, rather than dully exploiting it, I must launch into new ventures. . . . I feel a great desire to put off those who believe in me." And he did precisely that, traveling up to the Netherlands to view the work of the great Dutch masters and subsequently deconstructing some of them in his "Dutch Interiors." These paintings took apart works by Hendrick Martensz Sorgh and Jan Havicksz Steen and reassembled them in hilarious, erotic compositions. Later in his career Miró was at some pains to profess his reverence for the Dutch masters. It is impossible, however, to avoid seeing in his "Dutch Interiors" the spirit of a joyful artistic anarchy.

While he was influenced to some significant extent by Dada and Surrealism, Miró was far too much the radical iconoclast to own membership in any school or movement. Still, he couldn't escape the fact that he was part of an artistic avant-garde forty years and more in the making, whatever one wanted to call it. Beginning in the 1880s and based on philosophical and esthetic anarchism, artists of all kinds attempted the destruction of painting and sculpture as these had been known; of music and dance; of drama and poetry; and finally of film. The front line of this attack was Paris. There were the plays of Alfred Jarry (which presaged the "happenings" of the American 1960s) as well as his poetry, his polemics, and his destructive public behavior. The musical compositions of Erik Satie wickedly mocked classical form in their jarring juxtapositions of the stately and the comic. Henri Rousseau's paintings in their flat primitivism were defiant abrogations of centuries of artistic efforts in the direction of mimesis. Then there were Guillaume Apollinaire's poems that in their sometimes playful ambiguity teased the expectations of readers. André Breton was the self-anointed high priest of Surrealism, issuing manifestos and proclamations about what it was and wasn't. In his own work, the thrust was basically retrograde: trying to write out of some preconscious state, some place of dream or earliest childhood before calculation could mar the freshness of first perceptions.

Nor were these anti-art efforts simply that—against conventional notions of what constituted art. They aimed well beyond that, for whether in poetry or film, these artists wanted to inflict wounds on the collective psyche of contemporary culture, wounds that would bring to consciousness the rottenness of the modern world. Nothing better illustrated that rottenness than the ghastly waste of the Great War, the mendacity of its statesmen. Jarry, Rousseau, and others who lived in the prewar years had not seen what modern war could do. Those like Apollinaire, Satie, and the German painter George Grosz lived to learn it firsthand. To these artists only new and violently anti-art creations could possibly prove equal to the realities of the war and the cutthroat capitalism that came in its wake. Neither politics nor economics nor organized religion nor state educational systems reached deep enough to awaken humans to the world they had been prodded into as if at bayonet point.

If he hadn't gotten what *Un Chien Andalou* was all about—who had?—Miller did get the general thrust of the avant-garde movement, and references to it quickly began to crop up in his correspondence. In one of the Whitman-esque lists of sights and sounds he sent Emil (the Muslim section of Père Lachaise, pissoirs, Charlemagne's chess pieces), there is this:

Kandinsky, Lurcat, Miró, Czóbel, Dufresne
Surrealism—2nd Manifesto (Aragon, Breton, Soup-
ault, et alia)

Then, a few days later, he told Emil that when he finished his revisions on *Crazy Cock*, he thought he might also be finished with realistic literature. "I don't think it is the highest plane," he said.

What exactly the higher plane or planes might be and how to gain them would have to be for him a matter of personal investigation, experiment, and improvisation rather than through personal contact with avant-garde artists themselves and the possible cross-fertilization and inspiration that might have come out of that.[16] His one significant contact with a modernist in these early months, a visit to the studio of the Russian-French sculptor Ossip

Zadkine, had been pretty much a bust. He'd met Zadkine with June back in '28 but didn't really care much for him. Their second meeting went no better, with the sculptor and his other visitors chattering away in Russian, French, German, and Hungarian and only once in a while throwing the American the bone of an English word or two. So, even if he had chanced to be in the mood for one of his spontaneous monologues—and the setting was hardly right for that—the opportunity wasn't there for him: Miller was so radically American and still so very much the raw newcomer in France that his range of references would doubtless have been as incomprehensible to Zadkine and his friends as their languages were to him.[17] So, once again, he was reduced to being just a Brooklyn boy.

The encounter proved formative, and although it doesn't fully explain Miller's singular choice of comrades in Paris (or, later, in California, for that matter), it does help to explain why he made so very few really important artistic friends in France, while other American expatriates made many. The multimedia artist Man Ray (who also had a Brooklyn background), for example, knew just about everyone of any consequence in the arts during the '20s and '30s—Picasso, Matisse, Breton, Satie, Marcel Duchamp, Constantin Brancusi, Paul Eluard. He photographed Proust on his deathbed. He even got to know Henry Miller.

Hunger

So he was alone as far as artistic contacts were concerned. Instead he began to hang out a bit with streetwalkers of the seedier sort, the ones with rundown heels and rents in their stockings and bad teeth. He began taking notes on them, including dialogue. At first it may not have been evident to him that this could be literary material. What American writer of stature, after all, had written about whores, except Stephen Crane? And even there the writer hadn't really gotten close to how they worked and lived. At the outset, then, it may well have seemed more a matter of circumstance: he was drifting steadily downward to the point where it would have been natural, even inevitable, that he would encounter others in similarly hard-pressed circumstances.

He found things that were admirable in some of these women, especially their courage in a line of work more hazardous than that of Les Forts at Les Halles, more malodorous than that of the men who toiled through the night pumping the shit from the city's sewers and cesspools. The work of these women was not only hard and desperate, it was also hopeless, he found, and so once in a great while if he happened to have a couple of francs jingling in his pocket, he would treat one of them to a decent meal and a bottle of wine. It made him feel good to see some genuine color bloom in their cheeks, beneath the paint.

But his own circumstances were desperate enough and certain of his daily routines as apparently hopeless as theirs: his daily tramps over the river to the Right Bank, for instance, on his way to the American Express office where almost invariably he would be turned away. *Nothing for you this morning, sir.* He foresaw the looming possibility that if things went on this way, any sort of lodging would be beyond his reach, and he would have to camp out under bridges, in the bushes of parks, in crannies or alleyways: he saw people now so reduced. Already, he claimed to Emil, people were beginning to nudge each other when they saw him approaching, as if he were a *clochard*, a beggar. He wasn't that yet, and he would not become one, mostly because he proved to be a first-rate improviser with the guts of a second-story burglar.

For a while he arranged with a Russian émigré to sleep in the manager's office of the Cinéma Vanves. But even though the roof over his head was free, the air within its tiny, boarded-up confines wasn't: Miller felt more entombed than sheltered. He stood it as long as he could, then left: better to die in the open than to suffocate. He found food and lodging with another Russian in exchange for English lessons. (How his broad Brooklynese might have sounded issuing from Serge's mouth makes one pause.) But here again he found the domestic atmosphere very close and abruptly left. He found an expatriate painter from Brooklyn who had a studio he would let Miller sleep in for a few weeks. He ran into an East Indian he'd known from his Cosmodemonic days, a pearl merchant now somewhat down on his luck. And this man, too, took him in, not quite for old times' sake, but in exchange for Miller's services as his immediate body servant. The work was unpleasant, even slightly disgusting to this German-American, and what was worse was the food, which Miller found meager and profoundly unappetizing.

Then his fortunes changed when he chanced into Alfred Perlès, an Austrian writer he'd met through June. Perlès had a job on the *Chicago Tribune*'s Paris edition and was working on a Surrealist novel. The two men hit it off, and soon Miller had a new place to sleep when Perlès began slipping him past the concierge at his hotel in the Fourteenth. The neighborhood was an intensely interesting one for Miller, sitting behind Boulevard Montparnasse and its famous cafés. There was a lively outdoor market along Boulevard Edgar-Quinet, a street that ran past the entrance to the Cimetière du Montparnasse, within which was the tomb of Baudelaire. He too had been down-and-out here, writing of his rooms with their broken furniture covered in spittle and of the filthy windows down which the rain traced deep furrows.

Then there were the streetwalkers, some of whom brought their customers back to the hotel from Montparnasse, and Miller formed a friendship with one of them and began making extensive notes on her. In brief, life as a stowaway with Perlès was beginning to take on a sort of shape even if outwardly it looked as desperate as ever. He was after all still penniless and without prospects for any improvement in his situation. He had made no real headway on the revisions of his novels, though he had sent *Moloch* to a German publishing house and continued to work on *Crazy Cock*, which he had decided had a better chance at eventual publication. But he was now writing new things: about his streetwalker, the six-day bike races, and the Cirque Medrano. Eventually, his stories on these subjects would be published, giving him a certain small cachet.

Most important perhaps, he was learning how much he could do without, how one might organize a life stripped to its barest bones. Years back, Beatrice had given him a copy of Knut Hamsun's *Hunger*, a novel in which a nameless young writer comes to a city where he determinedly sets out to discover the outermost limits of suffering, how much of it he could bear. By the choices he makes he sinks into a ragged poverty, a starveling who stalks the streets with his intestines curling inside him like snakes. Hamsun refuses to tell us the why of all this, but now that he found himself in somewhat similar circumstances, Miller may well have begun to think of his life as a sort of experiment in creative deprivation instead of a ghastly accident. Maybe if you got all the way down and there wasn't anywhere else to go—except to the bottom of the Seine—then a kind of clarity might come to you, all choices having been removed from possibility.

June

Then June arrived on the first of her four disastrous visits. This was in September. He had warned her not to come without money, telling her (and Emil as well) that he couldn't possibly support the two of them. But she cabled some money and announced that she herself would soon follow. Clownishly, he missed her at the train station but then happened upon her at a café on Montparnasse, nonchalantly sipping a Pernod: June, with her incessant demands, her impossible expectations, her slovenly habits and maddening inconsistencies: here at last she was, grasping Val to her and breathily telling him she would never again allow him to suffer so. He fell for her all over again.

They went to the hotel they'd stayed at in 1928—and woke up in the morning covered with lice. Within days they'd begun to bicker, then to quarrel, and then to engage in pitched battles. But Val wasn't Val, she found, no longer the whipped cur she had sent away months ago. He had had a glimpse—fleeting, preliminary—of a new kind of existence here, with some kind of new work at its center. With June there, however, work was out of the question. Being with her was a full-time job, one that exhausted both of them, and after something less than a month she went back to the States for more money. As soon as she left Miller pulled himself together and began to reconstruct his life of severely disciplined poverty, one unencumbered and unclouded by June's fantasies, which from his new perspective he felt had completely engulfed her like the cigarette smoke she filled their room with each morning when she awakened.

What he needed now, he obscurely understood, was that bottom-dog clarity he had just begun to sense when she arrived, one where you were compelled to shed, one by one, your old illusions like worn-out items of clothing. Years later, looking back from America, he wrote in *The Time of the Assassins*, that every "renunciation has but one aim: the attainment of another level." If we put this later aperçu together with his remark to Emil about realistic literature not being the "highest plane," it becomes apparent that Miller was experiencing in these months what in religious literature has been called a "turning about in the seat of the soul." He had been forced to shed and shed, until he could feel the whole world beating against his skin. He still had a long way to go to feel this to such an extent that he could be free to be the artist he dreamed of becoming. But the way was there for him, even if it wasn't quite clear where it led.

In the immediate aftermath of June, he was at least clear-eyed enough so that he could tell Emil that he was deriving a savage glee from performing daily vivisections on *Crazy Cock*, "this novel that I've been dragging about from one hotel to another, across the ocean twice, thru bordellos and carnivals, a pillow at night in the movies, and under the bridges of the Seine. Stop! Cut the sentimentality!" Out, out, he went on, not raving now but writing with a ruthless abandon, "out with the apostrophes, the mythological mythies . . . the vast and pompous learning (which I haven't got!)." What he was meant to do, he told Emil, what he must do "before blowing out my brains, is to write a few simple sentences in plain Miller-esque language."

An Apache

With June gone Miller might have moved back in with
Perlès, but for some reason he didn't. Instead he moved
in with an American, Richard Osborn. Osborn was a Yale
Law School graduate working in a Paris bank. He was
also an aspiring writer living a double life, his days so-
berly spent at the bank and his nights consumed with bar-
hopping and chasing women in Montparnasse. Eventually this killing routine would catch up with him, but for
now he was managing it, though occasionally he'd show
up at the bank red of eye and with a rumpled suit. When
he happened to meet Miller he was taken with the raffish,
streetwise man who not only claimed to be a writer but
who actually seemed to be working hard at it. Osborn
sensed he had things to learn from Miller, both about

writing and about the tougher aspects of the city's night-
life. He had a large, cold flat on Rue Auguste Bartholdi
overlooking the drill grounds of the École Militaire in
the Fourteenth and offered Miller a space. In exchange,
Miller was to keep a fire going against the raw weather,
do a bit of cooking, and clean up around the place. The
fire wasn't a problem, and with his Germanic tidiness the
housekeeping wouldn't have been either—except most
mornings there was an awful lot of it to do. He and Osborn brought women home often, and after Osborn had
stumbled off to work in the morning, leaving Miller ten
francs on the dresser, Miller would have to go to work on
what sometimes looked like a shipwreck with bottles and
glasses strewn about, ashtrays overflowing, and scraps of
food found in odd places. It was a hell of a way to begin
his day—even if part of the mess was of his own making—
and he thought the stipend Osborn left him was nig-
gardly.[18]

But the flat was spacious and quiet, and he was working
again, still revising *Crazy Cock* but also working at the new
things—the bravely cheerful streetwalker he was calling
"Mlle Claude," the bike races, and the circus. When Osborn returned home at the end of the day, the pockets
of his overcoat clinking with bottles of Anjou, Vouvray,
Macon, the place was neat as a pin and the windows steamy

with heat. Miller was then ready to knock off work, for a while at least, to become Osborn's enthusiastic companion in the pursuit of women. But, said Osborn, when he himself had at last fallen into bed he could hear the tap-tapping of Miller's typewriter in the next room.

At this point, Osborn later recalled, Miller himself was ablaze like the stove, talking incessantly, brilliantly of the new literature that he was to be a part of, a literature that would be violently anti-literary, cracking apart all the old forms of expression. Through Miller's impassioned words, Osborn was brought to understand that his old gods— Conrad, Dostoyevsky—were already dated, "though still heroic landmarks." And Miller was talking this same way in his letters to Emil, telling him in mid-February 1931 that on a recent evening he'd brought home a copy of Mann's *Death in Venice* to bedazzle Osborn by reading it to him.[19] "And lo and behold! to my own absolute astonishment, I saw that Thomas Mann was dead . . . finished . . . *for me*." Thus, he continued, he was positively afraid to approach *The Magic Mountain* because he still believed in it and wasn't ready to shed that illusion too. Joyce also had lost his charm, and even his hero D. H. Lawrence now seemed oddly quaint with all his twaddle about social conditions in his novels when what he ought to have stuck to was simply "warmhearted fucking all the way through."

There remained only Proust and Spengler, a volume of whose works, so he told Emil, he had stolen from the American Library.

Another significant event of this winter was the development of a close, productive friendship with Brassaï. Gyula Halász had been a painter and journalist in his native Hungary before coming to Paris, where he took up photography under the name of his native village. Brassaï recalled that when they were introduced in December 1930, Miller's French was primitive while he himself had almost no English. But this didn't make any difference once Miller understood what the photographer was up to in his work, for here finally was someone who could understand—language or no—what he, Miller, was reaching toward but hadn't yet articulated. What Brassaï had embarked upon, Miller found, was a singular, solitary, immensely imaginative project: to document the city's secret life by night. Working by himself, he lugged his cumbersome equipment into the most recondite, forbidden, and sometimes actively dangerous corners of Paris to reveal what went on where most Parisians—including policemen —wouldn't dream of going, except in nightmare. Whereas Eugène Atget had famously documented the remnant architecture of an older Paris quickly passing away, and Brassaï's fellow Hungarian André Kertész had become an important member of the avant-garde, Brassaï was unlike either of these artists. Atget's focus was on the past, Kertész's on the future. Brassaï was interested in the now, the often brutal facts of daily life. He sought out the clochards who lived in the open in all kinds of weather. He followed the foul and dangerous work of the shit-pumpers. He hung out with the *apaches*, those roving gangs of pickpockets, burglars, strong-arm robbers, and street fighters. He haunted the emptied parks, the back streets, *bals musette* and pissoirs, the bridges and barges shrouded by night and fog. He got into whorehouses, lesbian clubs, homosexual ones, opium dens, the bell tower of Notre Dame at midnight. Several times he was physically threatened, had his equipment damaged, plates stolen. All of which endeared him to Miller, who wanted to learn what Brassaï had to teach him of those layers lying even beneath those he himself had experienced, those hidden infernos of vice and depravity and endless suffering. Brassaï showed him some of these, with Miller occasionally helping to carry the equipment. And there were a few areas of the city that the American had roved through, like the Thirteenth, that he was eager to have the photographer see. Looking at Brassaï's work made all these places come alive for the writer in a special way, for once the negatives had been developed in Brassaï's studio, blooming to life in the darkroom, suddenly they were *art*, an art he could aspire to equal in his own medium. Here the dark images of an underworld so filled with despair gave him instead both hope and heart.

Winter waned but the parties went on in Osborn's flat. An end of them was in sight, though, with the return of the owner in March. And so Miller would have to move yet again, but before that happened he would maximize his remaining days here—and hope he didn't die first or go blind from venereal disease: Osborn had picked up an alleged Russian countess and brought her home to live with them, but once there she announced she had the clap. Miller had been terrified of venereal disease by the public warnings about it he'd seen in his first days in the city— death's-head illustrations posted by the authorities in public bathrooms and pissoirs. Now with the countess's presence in the flat and her careless personal habits he was reminded of those grinning skulls. One day he made the ghastly discovery that he had used the countess's towel by mistake. She cheerfully assured him he couldn't go blind from that kind of contact, because if you could, she said, she would have lost her eyesight years ago.

So maybe it was just as well that the ménage à trois broke apart in March when Miller went to flop for a while in the studio of an American painter near the Cimetière du Montparnasse, his former neighborhood. He was hanging around a good deal with artists these days, he told Emil—Fred Kann, John Nichols, Sandy Calder—and finding the associations enriching. Yes, life was still as precarious as ever, but somehow it didn't seem to matter so much, and sometimes it didn't seem to matter at all. He felt, he told Emil in a March 10th letter, "exactly as all the great vagabond artists must have felt—absolutely reckless, childish, irresponsible, unscrupulous, and overflowing with carnal vitality." He didn't know where he'd have to go next, and he was missing quite a few meals. But life was rich in the things that really mattered, so much so that if he were told he must hang tomorrow, "I would say O.K. I've seen the show. And fuck you, Jack!"

Then this burst, not unbidden now but *earned*, even if it and the others that were to follow over the years would remain in some true sense mysterious:

Cafés, cemeteries, bistros in an orange light shedding a medieval aura of sanctity over the rubber black pavements. Prostitutes like wilted flowers and society dames glowing like gardenias. Pissoirs filled with piss-soaked bread and feuilletons of futile journalists sweating in cold garrets. Beyond the portes the "cold mournful perspective of the suburbs["]—by Utrillo, bastard son of Suzanne Valadon. The Seine running like a twisted knife between the Right and the Left

Banks. Sacré Coeur white in the night of Montmartre. Belgian steeds prancing with all their testicles thru the empty streets of midnight. Lesbians at the Dôme working off their excess lust in charcoal and ambergris. The Boulevard Jules Ferry still as a murderer's heart, emptying into the Abattoir de la Villette. Cold Greenland women at the Viking blazing under polar ice, their blonde wigs refulgent with exotic heat. A whore opposite me smiling lasciviously and scratching herself under the table. At the Rotonde, after three A.M., they lift up their dresses at the bar and run their fingers thru dark rose-bushes.

Superficially seen, the language here is not so different from that of Miller's earliest Paris letters in its piling up of disparate images. But those letters had been written in desperation, with a schoolboy's helter-skelter of, "I saw this and then I saw that and then I went home." This was not desperation (though surely the conditions described were desperate enough); this was artistic daring, the deliberate taking of risks to create an improvisation that would lift the writer and the reader above the quotidian Where and What to the existential Why. True, it was not yet a polished passage. But Miller wasn't after polish here—or thereafter for that matter. He was after words that when put together would hit the reader like a bullet or a bomb or, as he would say much later, like a "poisoned arrow." The passage does indeed make an impact even though it is a bit self-conscious in its use of words like "refulgent"; in its alliterations ("feuilletons of futile journalists"). Also, the influence of Whitman with his famous lists of urban sights and sounds and that of the Surrealists with their provocative metaphors feel a bit as if they are stuck on, applied.

Still, this is unquestionably new for Miller, in its language, its subject matter, and its tone and timbre. Here is the city's underbelly as he had come to know it, its armpits and groin and crotch—all evoked with a mixture of empathy as well as a merciless detachment. One is reminded again of Brassaï and his famous sequence, *A Man Dies in the Street* (1932), where the photographer, high above a rain-slick street, trains his camera on the scene below, where a man has dropped dead almost in the gutter. Brassaï keeps shooting as a crowd gathers, some under the shrouds of their umbrellas. They watch as the body is scooped up and loaded into an ambulance. And then they move on, leaving the scene as if nothing of moment had ever happened there. Brassaï invents nothing here, except the final selection of an eight-shot sequence from what may well have been a good many more than that. His aim, as in the nighttime photos of Paris, is acutely documentary in nature.[20]

His American friend and colleague greatly admired that detachment. But as a writer he wanted something more out of the same scenes Brassaï photographed: he wanted to see what was there, all right—the whores, the pissoirs, the cemeteries—but also what *might* be there, if only one could somehow cast off the blinders conventional culture had put on one. He wanted to see what was implicitly there, if only one could learn how again to use an imagination stunted and stifled by modern life. He didn't quite know how to do this yet, but this passage shows that he was learning, learning how to talk about what was revealed to him in his new and oftentimes terrifying freedom.

How he finally learned to do this is simple enough to state: he learned to write as he talked in those transports that sometimes would come upon him like a fit. This could have been the result of having been told often enough that this is what he ought to do, so that finally it sank in. Anecdotal evidence has Emil Schnellock telling him this back in New York when Miller was occasionally lighting up the studio with his brilliant bursts. Miller himself has June giving him substantially the same advice when she told him he'd be better off writing like himself instead of trying to ape his literary heroes. And then here in Paris we have the Lithuanian-born philosopher Michael Fraenkel repeating it when he heard Miller talking in the summer of 1931. The cumulative advice ought to have sounded good to Miller because he was a man who loved talk, his own and that of others: those tough-talking sports on the street corners of the Fourteenth Ward and those famous stem-winders Emma Goldman, Big Bill Haywood, and others whose cultural image went back to rural monologists and the heroically profane boatmen of the national folklore. Surely, these things went into his learning. But the alchemical process through which advice and example and cultural heritage must pass before these can become personal and therefore precious is rarely direct. Let us grant the importance of these factors and then add one more: his failure. For it was his solitary, heroic confrontation with this that proved decisive in the transformation of the man who called himself "The Failure" into the brilliant success he became with *Tropic of Cancer*, the most startling, scabrous passage of which is adumbrated in this March 10th letter to Emil.

For Miller had not come to Paris to find artistic freedom and rub elbows with his fellow artists. That had been the story of the expatriates of the 1920s. He had been exiled here as a failure, a failure as a writer and as a man. The longer he wandered the city's streets and haunted its poor quarters with their stinking bars and gurgling pissoirs, the longer he continued to slash at his manuscripts in this café and that, the more absolute his failure came to seem. Writing those rambling letters had a cumulative effect of objectifying this for him, forcing him to see how utterly false *Moloch* and *Crazy Cock* were to the man he was, how misguided his literary aspirations had been from the beginning. He had yearned to be a writer and an intellectual in the Old World mode, someone who would be respected anywhere. He was *not*, he had been furiously insisting for years, your average Joe from Brooklyn. But over these months in Paris, writing with an increasingly naked candor about his life, he came to see that in many ways that was in fact just what he was and that this was a good thing. For if he could capitalize on this, find a way to write out of the center of who he truly was instead of who he thought he ought to be, this would be the way forward for him. The letters helped him see this, for just as the personal letter can form the bridge between autobiographical experience and literature, so Miller's letters also served as a bridge between his past and his future, which would be the eternal *now*, this moment that he was living in a city that was anything but a City of Light, that was instead a City of Darkness, of ancient crime and despair and death. And yet, he hadn't gone under here. Instead, he had acquired a strange buoyancy, like one of those India rubber dolls that always pop back up no matter how hard you hit it.

Villa Seurat

The American writer Walter Lowenfels had been around Miller enough by early 1931 to be impressed by his cheerful resiliency, his belief in himself despite his shabby circumstances, his barren prospects. He mentioned Miller to Michael Fraenkel, telling the philosopher and book dealer that Miller might be an interesting example of the modern postmortem man, someone who had contrived a strategy for living creatively within the gigantic mausoleum both Lowenfels and Fraenkel believed Western civilization had become. Fraenkel was intrigued enough to invite Miller to his flat for an inspection, and Miller ended up staying until the middle of the summer.

Fraenkel's flat was at the end of Villa Seurat, a short *impasse* in a neighborhood of the Fourteenth that had become popular with artists. (Just behind Villa Seurat, there was a street called Rue des Artistes.) Dalí, André Derain, Antonin Artaud, and Tsuguharu Foujita had lived hereabouts, though, characteristically, while he stayed with Fraenkel Miller evidently had little if any contact with them. The area was seedy but just short of rough-and-tumble, a good place for meditative walks and with a brightly lit, capacious Alsatian brasserie nearby—just the sort of place Miller loved to work in.[21]

While he stayed with Fraenkel, Miller's duties were substantially those he'd had at Osborn's: to clean, to cook a bit, and to do some typing for Fraenkel. Also, to listen to Fraenkel, whose elaborate "death philosophy" Miller had drilled into him on a daily basis. Miller evidently didn't mind the philosophizing, and indeed a remnant of it eventually provided him with the opening lines of *Tropic of Cancer:* it was well worth it for a stable place to live and work, and during the daytime the place was quiet. But in addition to giving the impoverished transient a roof for a time, Fraenkel provided some other valuable services as well. For one thing, he read enough of *Crazy Cock* to confirm what its author had by now strongly suspected: that it was indeed vile crap. Fraenkel told Miller he should waste no more time trying to rescue it. His other service was more oblique but of greater importance.

Fraenkel was something of a people collector, one reason why Lowenfels had brought Miller to his attention. Fraenkel found the American an authentic character and remarkably representative of his culture, and in various ways he let him know this. Fraenkel may have been a crackpot, one-note philosopher, and later Miller would make savage fun of him. But at this delicately poised moment in Miller's artistic development, the cranky admiration this deeply cultured man had for him was highly important because it was a validation of what Miller himself had been moving toward in his letters home: that he was in truth an original, probably even an *ab*original. *You* are your own best subject, Fraenkel in essence told his guest: forget philosophy, forget being a thinker, forget the conventions of the novel. Just be yourself and write out of that.

For a while now Miller had been writing up his notes on Paris. At Fraenkel's, these scattered, random pieces began to take on shape and an idiosyncratic kind of coherency as Miller sensed they might make some kind of a book. He spent more time at the typewriter, less time wandering about, and still less time fussing over *Crazy Cock*.

When he was at the machine, he hammered at it with a ferocity that startled the visitors who dropped by at day's end to smoke, drink, and talk philosophy with Fraenkel. There in the midst of it all sat Miller at the machine, a cigarette in his mouth, a glass of wine at his elbow, typing away just as if he were in some tranquil setting—and perhaps for him now this was a species of tranquility. Alfred Perlès, who came around often, thought Miller might have been the fastest typist he'd ever seen, and Perlès had worked in a number of newsrooms. The painter Roger Klein recalled to Brassaï that Miller typing sounded like a machine gun, a simile that would have pleased the typist himself if Klein had repeated it to him. In another description, Klein said Miller reminded him of a "secretary practicing scales at a speed-typing competition." And the sheets that flew from the machine, Klein exclaimed to Brassaï: "Did you ever look closely at them? Not one erasure or type-over!" The stuff just poured out as if Miller had hooked a tap right up to the source. At that time when he felt he might very well be hot on the trail of something new, dangerous, and fearfully exciting, Miller might have been composing in the mode later made famous by Jack Kerouac and the Beats—"First thought, best thought." But despite what Roger Klein might have believed at that time, Brassaï knew that later his friend would spend many hours revising those pages that seemed to fly out of his typewriter.[22] For now, however, in Villa Seurat, Miller was in no mood for revisions. They could wait. When Fraenkel told him he was going to sublet the apartment, Miller moved back in with Perlès at the Hotel Central, and it was from there that he exultantly wrote to

Emil: "I start tomorrow on the Paris book: first person, uncensored, formless—fuck everything!"

Perlès came to Miller's rescue yet again at the end of that summer—someone was always there for him now it seemed—getting him part-time work at the *Tribune*. Working out of the basement of the paper's Right Bank building, Miller proofread stock market quotations. The paper was the poorest paying of the three English language dailies in Paris, and the work itself wasn't that much better than being a file clerk for the cement company in New York. Yet rather than being enraged by his evident lack of progress, Miller found that on the whole he rather enjoyed the job. For one thing, though the pay was meager, it was better than begging or feeling beholden in a daily way to someone, as he had been to Osborn. It gave him some walking-around money, and his needs remained minimal. Then too the work was almost completely mindless, leaving him the occasional odd moment to invent something in his head or to remember some detail, some incident of his life that he could potentially use. There were as well some interesting characters to hang out with after hours.

One was Wambly Bald, who turned out a daily column, "La Vie de Boheme," about the city's café life, one installment of which had in fact featured Miller, whom

Bald depicted as a sort of literary clochard whose only earthly care was to find a way to brush his teeth once in a while. Bald was a sour cynic with a broad streak of cruelty to his character. When Miller would put the touch on him—which happened often enough when Bald, Miller, and Perlès had knocked off work for the night—he might fling a few coins into the gutter for the pleasure of watching Miller retrieve them like a dog. He was equally cruel —and relentless—in his treatment of women, and after sating his cold lust on one of them he would detail the encounter to his companions, complete with unsparing characterizations of the meaninglessness of these experiences, how apt a metaphor they all were for the whole of life itself. Miller didn't appear to mind Bald's treatment of him any more than he minded Bald's treatment of women or his job: it was all grist for his mill now, as almost everything else was as well. He had become convinced that he could write, that he was in fact a real, honest-to-god writer, one who had an unshakeable hold on his subject: his life here and now on these desperate, crime-spattered streets. And so to dive into their gutters for a couple of centimes or to go up to Bald's flat to shine his shoes was fine. These experiences would find their ways into the Paris book and give it their gamy, gritty flavoring, like biting into a bit of buckshot in a savory rabbit stew.

He was still stalked by his fear of starvation and would

remain so for some time to come, but even here he had learned how to manage it and had recently improvised a scheme that in the short term anyway would supply some reassuring predictability to the eating problem. He had drawn up a list of friends and written to each of them, asking if they would be willing to give him a meal once a week, just one. Surely, he argued, this wasn't too much to ask. As it turned out, it was not, his friends being entirely willing, and so now Miller not only had his dinners taken care of, he also had yet another juicy piece of material to write up, joining it in a deliberately haphazard fashion to all the others he was piling up in those early morning hours when he and Perlès had at last arrived back at the Hotel Central while the market was beginning to wind down at Les Halles, the worn prostitutes might be meeting up with their *maquereaux*, their pimps, to settle accounts, and dawn was spreading itself over the roofs and chimney pots and spectral spires of the city.

At the end of September, June returned to Paris, and to Miller she appeared almost completely captive to her fantasies, which included a book she claimed to have just written called *Happier Days*. She was thinner, her clothes, too, and her skin was ashen. And to her Val was even more changed than she had found him on her previous visit, evidently no longer interested in *Crazy Cock*, which was to have been her monument, but talking excitedly instead of a new book about his life here. She instinctively disliked the sound of it. Val was also talking of a woman who he said might have potential as a patroness, but what he said about Anaïs Nin seemed to have more to do with ardor than art.[23]

It was Richard Osborn who had introduced Miller to Nin. Osborn worked in the same bank as Nin's husband, Hugh (Hugo) Guiler, and had done some legal work for Nin in connection with her recently completed study of D. H. Lawrence. Hugo began coming home with Osborn's tales of his picaresque companion who, so Osborn claimed, was destined for literary fame if he didn't die first. Nin had an appetite for the offbeat and the exotic, both of which she herself was, and soon enough she invited Osborn and his friend to the home the couple had at Louveciennes just outside the city. That evening she found Miller's behavior and manners a satisfying match for Osborn's colorful descriptions: he seemed to her a sort of genial savage with an astonishing lust for everything— food, wine, furnishings, the grass in the garden. In the diary she had been keeping since girlhood, she noted that Miller was "writing a book one thousand pages long which has everything in it that is left out of other novels." Shortly after this, when she had a chance to read something of his—on Buñuel—she found the writing "flam-

boyant, torrential, chaotic, treacherous, and dangerous."
Profoundly perceptive from an early age, Nin may well
have sensed this early that in Miller she had come across
the archetypal American her hero Lawrence had written
about, in his brilliant *Studies in Classic American Literature*,
whose soul was "hard, isolate, stoic, and a killer." Here was
a man who had somehow escaped the common delusions
of his native culture, the man who, so Lawrence had proph-
esied, would one day write something genuinely new, explosive. From what he told her, Nin knew that Miller
wasn't just talk, that he was even then attempting the perilous passage between literature as he had known it and a
literature that so far as he knew had yet to be written—
chaotic, treacherous, dangerous, savage. For her to be in
the company of such a man was thrilling. She was, for all
her rich and largely unsuspected interior life, living both
literally and metaphorically on the outskirts of the great
city where the artistic action was, to all appearances the
suburban housewife. And here, courtesy of the dissolute
Osborn, was a real renegade, dropped into her garden.
Showing him around it, she found herself wanting nothing so much as to assist him in his passage, to give him
things—money, a place to work. And she might also have
been thinking that here was a man who could inspire her
as well, who was emotionally prepared to understand her
own artistic aspirations and help her to realize them.

Whatever the precise nature of Miller's second dinner invitation may have been, when he came his wife came with him. "Henry came to Louveciennes with June," Nin wrote in her diary, and as June materialized out of the gloom of the garden, Nin said she "saw for the first time the most beautiful woman on earth. A startlingly white face, burning dark eyes, a face so alive I felt it would consume itself before my eyes."[24] Yet by the end of the evening June's erratic behavior, her obvious mendacity, had turned Nin away—but only temporarily. Shortly after this dinner, June returned to America, most likely to get additional funds from her admirers. But soon she was back, and the two women entered into a smoldering relationship that, if it never became physical, certainly went right up to the borderline. In an eerie reprise of what had drawn Miller to June, Nin was intrigued as much by the other woman's layers of disguise and mystery as by her unearthly beauty. She wondered whether what June really wanted most from the relationship was for Nin to write about her and so supply a corrective to what June feared would be Miller's slanderous fabrications in the new book he was so excited about. *Crazy Cock* had been disappointing enough. But whatever it was she was after and whoever she might be, June was a "superb and inspiring character," Nin felt, "one who makes every other woman insipid."

Once she understood that June was all artifice, one layer atop the next, Nin was free to surrender to her remarkable seductiveness without attempting to find the "truth" about the woman—a psychological maneuver Miller himself could never make. June was always talking, riddling, conspiring, her voice rich and breathless, her eyes drugged. By February 1932, with Miller down in Dijon with a miserable teaching job but continuing his courtship of Nin in voluminous letters and June once again back in the States, Nin could admit that she was trapped "between the beauty of June and the genius of Henry." In differing ways she found herself devoted to both of them, but "I love June madly, unreasonably. Henry gives me life, June gives me death. I must choose, and I cannot."

She was still feeling this way when Miller asked her for train fare back to Paris at the end of the month: he'd heard from Perlès that there was a full-time job waiting for him at the *Tribune*, and he was desperate to leave dreary Dijon for Paris and Nin. She sent him what he needed. Miller abruptly, unceremoniously left his teaching post, moved back into the Central, and took up his duties at the paper, working a night shift in the financial department. Within days of his return he and Nin were lovers.

The sexual part of the relationship bore certain resemblances to Miller's previous ones. But the sexual adventurer who had begun somewhat tentatively with the older Pauline Chouteau was by now well seasoned and knew what he wanted from a woman: plenty of action; acrobatics that might have provided useful additions to the *Kama Sutra;* and all of this accompanied by a steady stream of dirty talk that Nin for all her sophistication had not heard before. Certainly she had not heard it from her somewhat staid banker husband. It was shocking, something of an aphrodisiac, and psychologically soiling in its relentlessness. One afternoon after attending a concert by herself in the city, Nin felt cleansed by the experience, freed for the moment from Miller's world of "shit, cunt, prick, bastard, crotch, bitch . . ." Yet she was to willingly continue to be a denizen of that verbal and artistic underworld for another couple of years. It was as if she was compelled to live out the fictional career of Séverine Serizy, the wealthy Parisian housewife in Joseph Kessel's 1928 novel, *Belle de Jour,* who takes a perverse pleasure in the sadomasochistic tricks she turns by day in a whorehouse before returning each evening to her sedate marriage. The examples Nin records of Miller's talk leave nothing to the imagination. Neither does her description of a sexual encounter with him in the garden at Louveciennes where he suddenly attacked her, throwing her to the ground and making violent love to her. Miller the writer often wore the guise of civilized humanity, she wrote, but "that day I was fucked by a cannibal."

Throughout the relationship there were, of course, moments of great tenderness and trust as well as an artistic coupling that was productive for them both. But early on Nin doubted she truly loved Henry and thought she never would. Even her sexual climaxes with him felt somehow short of the high peak she so ardently sought. There was something in her lover that unsettled her in her soul, as if he really was a savage and not a human of her world. Maybe it was that his fierce, lonely struggles to make himself into a writer had stripped him not only of his pretensions and illusions but also of his basic humanity, leaving him *all* writer, *all* artist. Without his writing, she wrote in the fall of 1933,

I don't know what Henry would be. . . . People who know him as gentle, wonder at the writing. Yet sometimes I have the feeling that this gentleness is not entirely genuine. It is his way of charming. Of disarming. It allows his entry anywhere, he is trusted. It is like a disguise of the observant, the critical, the accusing man within. His severity is disguised. His hatreds and his rebellions. They are not apparent, or acted out. It is always a shock to others. I am aware at times, while he speaks in a mellow way to others, of that small, round, hard photographic lens in his blue eyes.

The entry is remarkable in several ways. To begin with, it is remarkably perceptive, especially when considered in context, for here, after all, was a woman with a substantial emotional involvement with this man, yet capable of drawing back to see him in pitilessly sharp detail. Clearly, she too had that photographic lens in her own eye. Then, her description of his hidden detachment gives us a glimpse of the Miller who had learned how to become a ruthless truth-teller, who had transmogrified himself from the self-indulgent, self-sorry literary oaf of *Moloch* and *Crazy Cock*, capable now of looking on scenes of bottomless depravity and despair without flinching or turning his head aside. Finally, Nin's snapshot of the merciless observer behind the mask of the New World rube reminds us of that broad, dark-hued swath of American folklore in which the isolate killer Lawrence had written about hides behind the laconic jokes of the Yankee, the robust jollity of the boatman, the comic qualities of Mose, the Bowery B'hoy.

The job at the *Tribune* didn't last long, but for once Miller didn't lose it because of his own negligence; instead he was a victim of the deepening Depression. However, he now had Nin who was happy to supply him with periodic cash gifts. These were sufficient to allow him and Perlès to move into a flat in the working-class district of Clichy. To Miller who had learned to love Paris's most sordid quarters the new neighborhood was dull, but Perlès loved it because to him it was wonderfully modern, and their apartment had comforts like separate bedrooms and up-to-date bathroom fixtures.

From Avenue Anatole France Miller once again trained his epistolary guns on Emil, writing that he now had solid financial assistance from a source he must not disclose and that this was allowing him to work full bore on what he was calling *The Last Book*. The manuscript, he said, rather resembled Emil's great accordion-like leather valise and into it he was throwing all manner of things, whether clean or soiled, ironed or pressed, tender or terrible. The order—or the disorder—was his to decide, and he had discovered that recklessness was his best artistic virtue. He would employ it to the utmost, even if it should ultimately cause him to be expelled from this country he had come to love. "I will never become a European," he said, "but thank God, I am no longer an American. I am one of those things you call an 'expatriate,' a voluntary exile. I have no country, no frontiers, no taxes to pay, no army to fight for." This last line in its defiant tone, its philosophical anarchism, as well as its cadence would survive all the versions of *The Last Book* to appear in the opening passage of *Tropic of Cancer*, though some of the wording would change. He was, he told his old friend, going for broke now, and when he had thrown everything that came to him into the valise—and broken all the rules—he would consider the thing finished and would dedicate it to Buñuel who had opened his eyes.

In the summer of 1932 friends put Miller in touch with William A. Bradley, a Paris-based agent who told Miller he would like to see the manuscripts of both *Crazy Cock* and *The Last Book*. Having finished the latter to his own satisfaction, Miller was at this point feeling the kind of postpartum depression not uncommon to writers, and hearing from Bradley—who was bound to seem to him an authority figure—further fouled his mood. Nevertheless, he did take the manuscripts to Bradley's office on the Ile Saint-Louis. As a point of honor he had made few if any cuts in *The Last Book*, and the stout valise was crammed to its capacity. Bradley replied in short order, telling Miller he would like to discuss the manuscripts with him, particularly *The Last Book*, which he found "magnificent." Miller's mood darkened yet further at this news: what he had really wanted to hear was that it was *Crazy Cock* that was magnificent and that Bradley would take it on. Instead, when he and Nin met with Bradley the agent dismissed *Crazy Cock* and said he wanted publisher Jack Kahane to see *The Last Book*. Evidently, Miller blurted out that *Crazy Cock* was the book he had been meant to write, while *The Last Book* was vastly inferior to it, was in fact a kind of afterthought. If June could have heard this and appreciated what a profoundly helpless tribute to her it was, she might have been grimly pleased, perhaps especially so since for some weeks thereafter Miller perversely persisted in trying to get both Bradley and Kahane interested in *Crazy Cock* while talking down *The Last Book*. Kahane hardly heard him. He was almost deliriously happy at the prospect of publishing *The Last Book* through his Paris-based Obelisk Press, since he regarded the book as a work of astonishing genius. He told both Bradley and Miller he could bring it out in February 1933. Gradually, Miller calmed down enough to sign a contract, though in his heart he still wanted Obelisk to first bring out *Crazy Cock*. In any event, *The Last Book* would be first, but it is significant that having signed on for *The Last Book*, he was reluctant to look at it and instead went to work on what eventually became *Tropic of Capricorn*, which would tell the story of his life with June in their early days. It is highly likely that had it not been for Nin he never would have done the work on the manuscript necessary to hammer it into the blazing, brilliant book Kahane eventually published, in English, in the autumn of 1934.

What She Gave

When in the 1960s the feminist movement in America expanded its consciousness beyond the national borders to embrace pioneering figures of other cultures, it was almost inevitable that Anaïs Nin would be "discovered" and perhaps exalted beyond even what she might have wished to claim for herself. But like the photographer-journalist Lee Miller, who began as the gorgeous mascot of the Paris Surrealists but emerged as an artist fully as interesting as many of them, Nin was for some decades known more as Henry Miller's sex kitten than as a formidable literary talent herself. Clearly, she would never for a moment have been willing to settle for that: her ego was as formidable as her talent. Still, for more than two years she did devote much of herself, body and soul, to Miller's

Tropic of Cancer because she saw within its gross disorder a great book. There was, she wrote in her diary at this time, "a splendor in his writing, a splendor that transfigures everything he touches," and to give this to the world was worth everything she had to go through. It was a lot, but she never lost her belief in the book. The question for her, however, was how she could apply the knife of her intelligence to the savage excesses of his imagination without cutting out what made *Cancer* completely unique. The task was, in every respect possible, daunting.

To begin with she had to deal with the seductive, spectral presence of the aboriginal muse, June, who at this most critical point reappeared for the final time. And now the contest between the two women took on a mythological valence, with June trying to kill off the new book and Nin, the new muse, trying to bring it to term—all the while partly sympathizing with June's position. As for Miller, he was of little help to Nin: June's untimely return had once again paralyzed him, and he was not to regain his emotional balance or his creative momentum for many months after she had departed for the final time at the end of 1933.

Years after *Tropic of Cancer* had at last seen print in September 1934, and at a point when its author appeared to regard it as a somewhat faded phenomenon that might have been the work of someone else, Miller looked back to 1933 as a period of "great fertility, great joy." It wasn't.

It is true that he was working on four literary projects during these months: the beginnings of what would become *Tropic of Capricorn;* an extended autobiographical meander that would be published as *Black Spring;* the revisions of *Cancer;* and a long essay on D. H. Lawrence that threatened to become a book and truly The Last Book— the last Miller would ever write. In addition, he was turning out a great number of primitivistic watercolors. Still, the available evidence indicates that despite this furious activity, his concentration on any of these projects was poor and he kept lurching from one to another in distracted fashion. He knew this, and made numerous programmatic resolves to settle into a more productive routine, but he could not.

For Nin the Lawrence project was the most worrisome. It was begun at the behest of Kahane, who had developed a big case of the jitters in the aftermath of his joyous acceptance of what Miller was now calling *Tropic of Cancer.* *Cancer* was so explosive, Kahane had come to feel, that something had to be done to soften its impact. His solution was for Miller to write something "legitimate" to demonstrate that he was not a pornographic writer—or a gangster author, as Miller had taken to calling himself. If Miller could turn out an extended essay on his old hero

Lawrence, it would introduce him to readers as a serious cultural critic while at the same time protecting Kahane against allegations that he was a smut peddler—which in fact he was.

In a kind of frenzy that probably had as much to do with his tangled feelings about *Cancer* as it did with any authentic enthusiasm for the project itself, Miller plunged into Lawrence, and very quickly the monograph became a monstrously bloated thing, replete with many of the very literary faults he'd told Emil almost three years back he was through with: his aspirations to write great literature in the classic Continental mode; his propensity to vast divagations; his philosophical pretensions; his beerhall sentimentality. By then June had departed, and in that way at least the field had been cleared a bit, so Nin had Henry to herself. But she had no control over the conditions Kahane had set and Miller had accepted. And so she could do little more than watch from the sidelines while Miller read more and more, receding into the far reaches of the history of the West, creating giant schemas that would explain Lawrence—and everything else as well in the full Spenglerian mode. At last in the summer of '33 she told him he wasn't really a philosopher, an intellectual, a thinker—precisely what Miller had confessed to Emil he knew he wasn't. Instead, he was a *writer*, an artist gifted with an extraordinary imagination. *That* was what he ought to be cultivating and what she wanted to nurture.

In February 1934, still stalled on all fronts and Kahane still delaying publication, Miller chucked everything and left Clichy to join Nin in Paris's high-toned Passy neighborhood, where she had taken a flat so she could more conveniently see her psychoanalyst Otto Rank. Apparently it was there that she finally succeeded in convincing Miller that what he needed most to do at this crucial point was to focus all his creative energies on *Cancer* and that she could help him. She could see how the book might be trimmed and tightened and that the process would not require the sacrifice of the "truth." During the winter months and on into the spring the two went at it, Miller fighting to preserve all the excesses and meanders and extraneous elements that were to him the dearest things in the manuscript, precisely because they most evidently involved his escape from psychological and esthetic tyranny into anarchical freedom. Already the thing was becoming a stranger to him as he read through the pages of a second and then a third revision, and he found it hard to believe he'd endured such suffering in order to write it. He wrote Emil that he knew he would never write another book like it.[25] By the time Kahane had at last put the book in press —without the stalking-horse of the Lawrence project— Miller was pretty well fed up with the whole business and

wrote Emil that he got more of a kick out of looking at one of his botched watercolors than at reading his page proofs.

At summer's end he learned that an airy, roomy studio until recently occupied by Antonin Artaud in the Villa Seurat was available. It was upstairs from Fraenkel's former flat. Doubtless with Nin's financial assistance, Miller jumped at the opportunity to live on the very spot where so many significant realizations had come to him. And even if he was in some inward way estranged now from *Cancer*, he knew that in taking up residence here he had come a very long way. On the day he took possession of the flat, Kahane appeared at the door with the first copies of the book (perhaps he was afraid to mail it). Walter Lowenfels had donated a Victrola and a stack of recordings —jazz, classical music. But what Miller most wanted to listen to in this crowning moment were the sentimental airs of Stephen Foster.

The day following, Miller and Nin prepared copies for mailing. Beneath the innocuous wrappings, the book's physical appearance was fully as forbidding as even the "gangster author" himself could have wished: a compact soft-cover item bearing on the front a drawing of Cancer, the zodiacal crab, carrying in its horny claws the body of a woman, either dead or ravished. It was the work of Kahane's fourteen-year-old son, much later to be Miller's publisher. Wrapped around it like a *préservatif* was a two-inch-wide paper band warning,

FOR SUBSCRIPTION.

MUST NOT BE TAKEN INTO

GREAT BRITAIN OR U.S.A.

The front flap copy compared the book to Céline's *Journey to the End of the Night*, while the back flap advertised other books available from Obelisk, including three by Kahane, writing under the pseudonym Cecil Barr: *Amour French for Love; Bright Pink Youth;* and *Daffodil*, "A young girl's amorous adventures in the Paris of to-day." For a writer so militantly anti-establishment and who had said in the book that his aim was to get off the "gold standard of literature," Miller's behavior with his brand-new book was fairly conventional, sending copies off to numerous literary luminaries and friends on both sides of the Atlantic. By this point his hatred of America, both social and cultural, had risen to hysterical proportions—but he still wanted to be noticed over there, even if invidiously so.

1934

In this year, the self-proclaimed heavyweight champion of American letters, Ernest Hemingway, was putting the finishing touches on a short story collection, *Winner Take Nothing.* It contained some of Hemingway's most enduring work—"The Gambler, The Nun, and the Radio," "The Light of the World," and especially "A Clean, Well-Lighted Place." Still, the already legendary tough guy found himself having to make certain unhappy concessions to what was permissible in mainstream American publishing. In the manuscript version of "The Light of the World," for example, a teenager named Tom says to a bartender who is giving him some trouble, "'Up your ass.'" In the published version this came out as, "'You know where.'" In "A Natural History of the Dead," an artillery lieutenant says to a field surgeon, "'Fuck your-self.'" And "'Fuck your mother. Fuck your sister . . .'" These were published as "'F——.'" Hemingway had ar-gued for his originals, but his editor, the eminent Max-well Perkins, had at last gotten him to listen to reason. Plainly, literary modernism even at its toughest had its cultural limitations. One could write about war with psy-chological candor, as Hemingway had in the collection's "A Way You'll Never Be." But an unsanitized depiction of the hideousness of war—the same war that had so aroused Surrealist reaction—was in the final reckoning substan-tially prohibited because the language that would have been fully appropriate to the phenomenon itself was judged offensive—more offensive evidently than the war itself.

Something of the same situation applied to F. Scott Fitzgerald's *Tender Is the Night,* published in the same year, where the root of the heroine's psychological problems is her incestuous relationship with her father. The attentive reader could be in no doubt as to what had happened be-tween father and daughter, and yet the whole affair and its consequences are handled with a delicacy and remove that makes Nicole Diver's reactions seem excessive and bizarre rather than tragic and understandable.

In 1934 William Faulkner was in full creative stride and beginning to ponder with renewed seriousness a theme he had been considering at least since 1931: incest (again) as a metaphor for the entire experience of the American South. But while the threat of incest is the fulcrum of the plot of *Absalom, Absalom!* published two years later, it remains far more a brooding metaphor than an unspeakable physical fact. Which, to be sure, would not be to say anything germane about the novel's qualities, for indeed it has a strong claim to being the Great American Novel, that mythic beast. It is to say, however, that Faulkner knew full well the cultural conventions of his time and place and indeed had suffered critically for having violated them in *Sanctuary* (1931), in which his heroine is raped with a corncob. In *Absalom, Absalom!* he chooses to leave the brother-sister relationship just short of incest, perhaps as a necessitous tradeoff that would allow him to deal in these pages with the even greater taboo of miscegenation.

In 1934 Thomas Wolfe was at work on *Of Time and the River,* a sequel to *Look Homeward, Angel,* and James T. Farrell, who had himself endured a year of poverty in Paris in 1931, published a sequel to *Young Lonigan* as *The Young Manhood of Studs Lonigan.* This post-Naturalism novel of lower-class life in Chicago features racial violence, torture, alcoholism, and venereal disease—rough stuff indeed. But in many respects the novel could have been written at the turn of the century, and despite its subject matter neither author nor publisher faced any real threat from the censors or the courts.

Farrell regarded himself as a rebel, writing against the establishment, and in some respects he was. But not in comparison with Miller in *Tropic of Cancer*. For in fact, *Cancer* was artistically far more daring, more uncompromising, more radically American than anything published by Miller's illustrious contemporaries in that year—and for many years thereafter as well. Even in 1961, the year of its American publication, it still looked amazingly avant-garde, enough so that its appearance through Barney Rosset's Grove Press was a cultural sensation felt far beyond the realm of arts and letters. It was in truth one of the first major shots fired in what were to become the cultural wars of that remarkable decade.[26]

Half a century and more since that epochal event the book can still hit the unsuspecting reader like a sledge-hammer or a bomb or a kick below the belt, and this despite tectonic cultural shifts in the permissible public treatment of sex and sexuality. Movies, television, dance, drama, the lyrics of popular songs—all these now deal with the formerly forbidden in remarkably frank fashion. And at suppertime, televised ads (the province of the artistically thwarted) bring to our living rooms their tiny dramas of rectal ailments and penile malfunctions. Nobody bats an eye at these oddly cheerful depictions of the old-time unmentionables. In literature, writers like Jean Genet, Hubert Selby Jr., William Burroughs, Allen Ginsberg,

J. P. Donleavy, and James Purdy have followed the path Miller blazed in *Tropic of Cancer,* and more recently an English-born novelist, Charlotte Roche, has achieved a Milleresque notoriety for her *Wetlands,* which describes in exquisite detail its teenaged heroine's exploration of her body and how to arouse its most intense erogenous capacities through the use of shower heads, avocado pits, razors, and the like.

Form

Emil Schnellock's accordion-like valise that Miller had invoked in his letter of spring 1932 was only a metaphor of the moment for him as he tried to explain to himself what he was trying to do in *Tropic of Cancer:* throwing *everything* into it in the effort to get down on paper for once the fantastic essence of living—"caviar, rain drops, axle grease, vermicelli, liverwurst," as he eventually was to put it in the novel itself. This wasn't to be a *life*, which to him evidently had a finished quality to the very sound of it, as if it had been composed in tranquility or even done by somebody other than the subject himself. No, this was to be a book about *living*, the quick, quivering beat of it. Others had talked of doing this, he knew, and there were certain passages in Whitman that had captured this quality, those where the man had flung aside form and all the current conventions of prosody and had written from the heart's chambers. Wambly Bald, Miller's drinking and whoring companion, was always threatening to write a book in which he would fling himself on the operating table and rip open his guts. But somehow he never quite got around to doing so: there was always another book to be consulted, always another beer to finish first, as Waverly Root had acerbically observed. It really took something, Miller discovered, to make such an attempt, to take that imaginative leap out into the artistically unknown.

How much he knew of Emerson at that point is a question. He certainly knew enough to appropriate an Emersonian line as his inscription to *Cancer:* "These novels will give way, by and by, to diaries or autobiographies—captivating books, if only a man knew how to choose among what he calls his experiences that which is really his experience, and how to record truth truly." Much later, as an inscription for *The Books in My Life*, he made use of another line of Emerson's: "When the artist has exhausted his materials, when the fancy no longer paints, when thoughts are no longer apprehended, and books are a weariness—he has always the resource to *live*." What Miller valued in these lines was the great man's strong preference for personal experience over artifice, for works that drove headlong toward the heart of living, works that were heedless of form, of artistic convention, of decorum, shapeliness, even common sense. "The way to write is to throw your body at the mark when your arrows are spent." This line could be Miller's but is not: it is Emerson's.

This is in fact what Miller does in *Tropic of Cancer*, and far more than the reiterative use of such words as "cunt" and "fuck," it is what keeps the book vibrant and fresh, even in an age as jaded as our own.[27] Art, Miller had come passionately to believe in the crucible of his Paris apprenticeship, "consists in going the full length." As he worked on *The Last Book*, at first in fumbling fashion and then with an increasing confidence that became finally the folkloric boatman's boastful bravado, he looked over his shoulder at his old literary heroes and found that the things he had most loved in them were their excesses—structural, stylistic, moral. "When I think," he writes midway through *Cancer*, "of their deformities, of the monstrous styles they chose, of the flatulence and tediousness of their works, of the obstacles they heaped up about them, I feel an exaltation." Their terrible excessiveness, he continues, "is the sign of struggle, it is the struggle itself with all the fibers clinging to it, the very aura and ambiance of the discordant spirit." These were the "great and imperfect ones" whose very confusion and incoherence were divine music to those like himself who had ears to hear. The true artist, the one who throws himself at the target when his last

arrow is spent, "must stand up on a high place with gib-
berish in his mouth and rip out his entrails." Any art that
fails to go this last full measure, that falls short of this
"frightening spectacle, anything less shuddering, less terrifying, less mad, less intoxicated, less contaminating is
not art."

The standard Miller sets himself here is, to be sure,
heroic and heroically impossible, as his own language
makes clear in this passage. It is what we hear in the best
of jazz, America's classical music, when it roars deliberately into dissonance. And yet. And yet Miller comes astonishingly close: *Tropic of Cancer* goes the full length. And
whatever may be thought about the range of its language,
its passages of tediousness and incoherence and a density
that comes close to an impenetrable obscurity, it was
unprecedented in its own time and is still challenging in
our own.

It begins with talk of body lice, with insults to the reader,
and with an obscene love song to a woman named Tania.
It ends with the narrator down by the banks of the Seine,
contentedly counting out the money he has stolen from a
friend. In between there are:

—Non-sequential fragments of life at the Villa
   Borghese, which turns out not to be the papal pile

in the hills outside Rome but an apartment in a seedy section of Paris occupied by a gang of characters not identified in any meaningful way. Life here seems to be coming to an end—the flat is to be sublet. But this may be a metaphor for life in the whole of Western civilization itself: the cancer of time and internal rot is eating the West away.

—The narrator's notes on a wandering, impoverished life in Paris. What keeps him going is the writing of a book that he intends to be scandalous in the extreme, a "prolonged insult, a gob of spit in the face of Art." He has a wife, but she is out of his life now, and he feels completely free to pursue numerous sexual adventures, a few of which are treated with considerable tenderness but the vast majority played for their crudely comic potential.

—Slices, served up here and there, of continental history: the Black Death; the ghastly circumstances of the life of Charles VI, Charles the Mad, a verminous prisoner within his own walls where he played cards with his only companion, the baseborn Odette Champdivers.

—Intimate encounters with the Parisian demimonde, the hookers, their maquereaux, and their customers; their café hangouts and behavior; the streets, alleyways, and *impasses* where the women lie in wait for their johns. The intersection, for instance, of Pasteur-Wagner and Rue Amelot, "which hides behind the boulevard like a slumbering lizard."

> Here at the neck of the bottle . . . there were always a cluster of vultures who croaked and flapped their dirty wings, who reached out with sharp talons and plucked you into a doorway. Jolly, rapacious devils who didn't even give you time to button your pants when it was over. Led you into a little room without a window usually, and, sitting on the edge of the bed with skirts tucked up gave you a quick inspection, spat on your cock, and placed it for you.

—Portraits of the narrator's companions: Carl (Alfred Perlès); Van Norden (Wambly Bald); Fillmore (Richard Osborn); Boris (Michael Fraenkel); Cronstadt (Walter Lowenfels); Marlowe (Samuel Putnam, an expatriate publisher); Tania (Bertha Schrank, wife of a playwright); and Mark Swift (American painter John Nichols). Anaïs Nin is nowhere even alluded to, for very practical reasons. For the most part the portraits are hardly flattering, the narrator observing these people through that hard photographic lens of which Nin had written. Many of them are funny in the morally

and emotionally costly way traditional American
humor can be.

—Also, portraits of individuals the wandering narrator crosses paths with and who provide him with
food, shelter, temporary employment, or simply
literary material: Eugene, an émigré Russian piano
player in a cinema (Eugene Pachoutinsky); Serge,
another Russian émigré, who delivers disinfectant
to commercial establishments (not otherwise
identified); Nanantatee, an Indian pearl merchant
(N. P. Nanavati); an unnamed photographer who
takes pornographic photos to be sold in Germany
that the narrator poses for (Brassaï); Macha, an
alleged Russian princess who lives for a time in
a flat with Fillmore and the narrator (a woman
variously remembered as either Sonya or Irene).

—Philosophical excursions, some occasioned by the
narrator's picaresque misadventures, others by
inner promptings. Some border on the hallucina-
tory while others are scabrous. And some are both
of these at once. Such is the case with one provoked by a drunken carouse at Fillmore's flat with
two streetwalkers who are performing naked acrobatics on the living room floor. When one of the
women turns a somersault and almost lands in the

narrator's face suddenly the orgy becomes a moment of cosmic clarity for him in which a "cunt" is seen as an awful metaphor for the universal debasement we call life. "When I look down into this fucked-out cunt of a whore," the narrator says, "I feel the whole world beneath me, a world tottering and crumbling, a world used up and polished like a leper's skull. If there were a man who dared to say all that he thought of this world there would not be left him a square foot of ground to stand on." Here is the monstrous condition the eons of human existence have brought us to: two drunken men and with them two desperate women who are literally turning tricks for a few francs—the moral equivalent of the biblical thirty pieces of silver. And it is not simply this foursome that is so lost; the whole world is sliding toward doom and someone has to have the guts to say so:

> It may be that we are doomed, that there is no hope for us, *any of us*, but if that is so then let us set up a last agonizing, bloodcurdling howl, a screech of defiance, a war whoop! Away with lamentation! Away with elegies and dirges! Away with biographies and histories and libraries and

museums! Let the dead eat the dead. Let us
living ones dance about the rim of the crater,
a last expiring dance. But a dance!

—Numerous Paris street scenes, the products of the
narrator's necessarily nomadic existence, bounced
from one shabby hotel to an even shabbier one;
from one free room—often enough merely the
floor for a bed—to the next; walking the night-
shrouded streets, some of which remind him of
nothing less than a big "chancrous cock laid open
longitudinally," with his empty guts growling:

wandering along the Seine at night, wandering
and wandering, and going mad with the beauty
of it, the trees leaning to, the broken images in
the water, the rush of the current under the
bloody lights of the bridges, the women sleeping
in doorways, sleeping on newspapers, sleeping
in the rain; everywhere the musty porches of the
cathedrals and beggars and lice and old hags full
of St. Vitus' dance; pushcarts stacked up like
wine barrels in the side streets, the smell of
berries in the market place and the old church
surrounded with vegetables and blue arc lights,
the gutters slippery with garbage and women in
satin pumps staggering through the filth and

vermin at the end of an all-night souse. The
Place St. Sulpice, so quiet and deserted, where
toward midnight there came every night the
woman with the busted umbrella and the crazy
veil; every night she slept there on a bench under
her torn umbrella, the ribs hanging down, her
dress turning green, her bony fingers and the
odor of decay oozing from her body.

—An excursion to teach at a *lycée* in Dijon, a position
and a town the narrator finds more desolate than
even the most hopeless quarters of Paris, the whole
place stinking of mustard that is "turned out in
carload lots, in vats and tuns and barrels and pots
and cute-looking little jars." The school itself
appears to be an "inverted mountain that pointed
down toward the center of the earth where God or
the Devil works always in a straitjacket grinding
grist for that paradise which is always a wet dream."
Here is hardly an escape from the precariousness
of Paris, only another kind of purgatory.

—A final extended vignette of the American expatriate Fillmore, who has fallen into the clutches of a
violently possessive hooker who convinces him he
has gotten her pregnant. The narrator is hardly
a good Samaritan, but he smells a rat here and

persuades Fillmore to withdraw all his money from the bank and do what he so desperately desires— run away to America. Fillmore finally agrees on the condition that the narrator promises to deliver to the girl the substantial payoff Fillmore hands him. The narrator does promise, but as soon as Fillmore totters aboard the train, the narrator pockets the cash and takes a leisurely cab ride to the side of the Seine, where he sits down to muse on his ill-gotten gain and on the great river, flowing always past just this spot, onward toward the sea.

The Grounds of Great Offense

This is to be sure a great, bloody sprawl of a book, as Miller himself surely knew, even after three extensive rewrites. When in these pages he imagines a bewildered reader of Whitman exclaiming, "Holy Mother of God, what does this crap mean?" he might well have been talking about *Tropic of Cancer*.

He knew that it was an assault on received notions of structure and plot, an assault on the taste, the patience, and the expectations of even the most adventurous of readers. But then, he'd never wanted it to be a novel, nor even a book really. (In effect he'd settled for the physical form it had to take—papers bound together.) Instead, he had wanted it to be an *event* that wounded and scarred, that was in every possible respect a profound and continuing

offense for which no forgiveness was possible. The fact
that the book remained outlawed for more than a quarter century was to be a continuous source of satisfaction
to him.

It was of course the language that gave greatest offense.
But it wasn't only the language. It was also the *tone* of the
thing, the fact that the most outrageous, even criminal
behavior was related with a certain cheerfulness that com-
pounded the offense of the obscene language. A slavering
pornographer by comparison looked better: such perverts
must be punished, of course, but after all they were fairly
easily identified and marginalized. This was different. This
seemed not to titillate so much as to take a fiendish delight
in rubbing the reader's face in filth just for the pleasure of
it. What after all could be said of a writer who detailed
with evident relish the ins and outs of the sex trade? How
could a man of considerable learning describe with such
pleasure the one-legged whore standing watch on her
wooden stump at the entrance to a hellish alleyway and
then cap so pathetic a scene with a crude joke about the
danger of getting splinters when taking her to bed? What
sort of writer would devote several pages to the ghastly
spectacle of his friend's prolonged, passionless assault on
a streetwalker, even to the point of getting down on hands
and knees behind him to witness its most intimate details
while tickling his friend's rear end from time to time? All

this was beyond pornography. This was positively inhuman, bestial—a characterization that the narrator in fact joyfully anticipates and accepts.

Nor was this tone confined to sexual matters. Almost any subject could be treated similarly, such as the case of poor Peckover, a miserable proofreader at a newspaper who falls down an elevator shaft at the plant and dies of his injuries—but not before blindly groping about on broken knees searching for his new set of false teeth. The news of the death of their colleague is subsequently related to the narrator and Van Norden in a bar by one of the paper's big shots, an "upstairs man," who spares none of the details. When he has finally finished and wandered off with his drink, the narrator and Van Norden laugh themselves silly over the false teeth.

> No matter what we said about the poor devil, and we
> said some good things about him too, we always came
> back to the false teeth. There are people in this world
> who cut such a grotesque figure that even death renders them ridiculous. And the more horrible the death
> the more ridiculous they seem. It's no use trying to
> invest the end with a little dignity—you have to be
> a liar and a hypocrite to discover anything tragic in
> their going. And since we didn't have to put on a false
> front we could laugh about the incident to our heart's

content. We laughed all night about it, and in between times we vented our scorn and disgust for the guys upstairs, the fatheads who were trying to persuade themselves, no doubt, that Peckover was a fine fellow and that his death was a catastrophe. All sorts of funny recollections came to our minds—the semicolons that he overlooked and for which they bawled the piss out of him. They made his life miserable with their fucking little semicolons and the fractions which he always got wrong. They were even going to fire him once because he came to work with a boozy breath. They despised him because he always looked so miserable and because he had eczema and dandruff. He was just a nobody, as far as they were concerned, but, now that he was dead, they would all chip in lustily and buy him a huge wreath and they'd put his name in big type in the obituary column. Anything to throw a little reflection on themselves; they'd make him out to be a *big* shit if they could. But unfortunately, with Peckover, there was little they could invent about him. He was a zero, and even the fact that he was dead wouldn't add a cipher to his name.

Of this and many kindred episodes it might merely be observed that we are confronted here with examples of that peculiar brand of cruel humor spawned in America by the

repetitive hardships of subduing a wilderness continent—
the kind exemplified by Mike Fink's blank-faced question
after he'd murdered his friend, Carpenter, "Is the whiskey
spilt?" And this would be true. It would also be true that
Miller himself was personally inclined toward humor of
a crude and violent sort and had been laughing at dirty
jokes, dirty words, stories of gruesome deaths, pratfalls,
burlesque, and the like for most of his forty-three years.
But something more is involved here, something that
leads us into the heart of the book.

When we give the Peckover episode a bit of reflection,
we find that what is truly shocking about it is not the
manner of his death. Nor is it even his erstwhile colleagues' hysterical laughter over the circumstances—the
false teeth and so on. No, what is shocking, what STAYS
shocking, is Peckover's *life*, the daily humiliations of it,
the inhumanity of it—his coat held together with pins; his
termagant wife terrified of what will become of them if he
lost his job; the daily loads of shit he had to put up with to
keep it (availing ourselves here of the narrator's diction):
this is what is shocking. This and the fact that such a life
is not even unusual, is in fact awfully ordinary, for Peckover is only a solitary case we happen to hear of out of the
many millions just like it. This is what earthly existence
has become for most of us in the world we have made. In
this cosmic overview Progress appears to be a cruel hoax

because the demeaning, hazardous conditions of human existence never truly change, whether we live in skyscrapers with central heating or hovels warmed with the dried dung of ruminants; whether we communicate across a great city by *pneumatique* or by barefoot traders bearing goods and messages between villages; whether we travel by horseback or jet. In the narrator's view these difference are incidental, for we are all versions of poor Peckover who has to put up with so much shit before he has the good fortune to fall down an elevator shaft and find a sort of release at the bottom of it. "For the man in the paddock," Miller's narrator says, changing only the circumstance, "whose duty it is to sweep up manure, the supreme terror is the possibility of a world without horses. To tell him that it is disgusting to spend one's life shoveling up hot turds is a piece of imbecility. A man can get to love shit if his livelihood depends on it, if his happiness is involved."

Why is this awful irony so? Why are Peckover and the man in the paddock with his rake and shovel and wheelbarrow willing to put up with so much shit? The answer Miller supplies in these pages is that they are willing because they believe that somewhere down the miserable road they call their lives there lies an exit, a way out, something or other that will redeem all their sufferings and make of life a glorious thing at last.

This point is made in another episode of equal pungency in which the narrator takes a young Hindu to a whorehouse at the young man's request. He is in Paris on his way to England to spread the gospel of Gandhi, and the ascetic robes have begun to hang very heavily on his youthful frame. Up in the room with the girl, the young man mistakes the bidet for a toilet and deposits into it "two enormous turds." The girl is aghast, the madam furious, the young man mortified. But the narrator remains coolly observant and is able to calm everyone down—a lamentable mistake, perhaps some extra money for the girl, some more for the maid. . . . Days later, the narrator is guiding the same young man around the city when another moment of cosmic clarity overcomes him as he thinks back on the incident: what if after everything is said and done human existence should come down to just those "two enormous turds which the faithful disciple dropped in the *bidet*."

> What if at the last moment, when the banquet table is set and the cymbals clash, there should appear suddenly, and wholly without warning, a silver platter on which even the blind could see that there is nothing more, and nothing less, than two enormous lumps of shit.

Scabrous, yes. Shocking still? Even today this is an image of the End of Days one is unlikely to forget soon. And as with the death of Peckover and the plight of the man in the paddock, this is the same point made in the same way: in some terrible way human beings over eons have collaborated in creating conditions of earthly existence that are truly execrable. From birth to death it is little more than a senseless scramble, sustained only by the hopeless hope that somewhere there will be a miraculous escape from it. "One is ejected into the world like a dirty little mummy," the narrator says. And all the roads are

> slippery with blood and no one knows why it should be so. Each one is traveling his own way and, though the earth be rotting with good things, there is no time to pluck the fruits; the procession scrambles toward the exit sign, and such a panic is there, such a sweat to escape, that the weak and the helpless are trampled into the mud and their cries are unheard.

And all of this, he says, is because of the human refusal to accept, or, better, to come to creative terms with, the inescapable conditions of earthly existence: birth, toil, suffering, aging, loss, death.[28]

The fundamental conditions of life (read, "shit") cannot be changed, but the narrator believes that what might be altered is our attitude toward life as it is. It is not, therefore, that men have created roses out of this dung heap, but that, for some reason or other, they should *want* roses. For some reason or other man looks for the miracle, and to accomplish it he will wade through blood. He will debauch himself with ideas, he will reduce himself to a shadow if only for one second of his life he can close his eyes to the hideousness of reality. Everything is endured—disgrace, humiliation, poverty, war, crime, *ennui*—in the belief that overnight something will occur, a miracle, which will render his life tolerable.

And while all is endured, as with poor Peckover, hung up between the Scylla of home and the Charybdis of the job; or the nameless toiler in the dung heap of his paddock; or the disciple with his aspirations, his secret lusts, his affectations—all this while time is there in the background, "beating away like a meat axe."

A New World

At the very outset of *Tropic of Cancer* the narrator says that
he has been sent to Paris "for a reason I have not yet been
able to fathom." Placed thus, the remark seems a trifle
obscure, but then, in these opening pages there are more
than enough obscurities—who *are* these people and why
are we being told these things about them?—so that it
does not seem to merit special attention. By the book's
last pages, though, it has acquired a resonance, for the
narrator's journey, which is in a real sense Henry Miller's
own, is just this process of fathoming, like the leadsman
on Twain's Mississippi who would literally sing out the
depths and so mark the boat's perilous passage along the
river's mighty seaward flow. Miller's narrator has been
sent—in the sense of something forced, necessitous—on

an exploration not of the river but of the wilderness of the city: the sinister twists of its ancient streets, which often enough end in culs-de-sac; the sewer-like stretches lined with bars and waiting women, and the bleak boudoirs of the hotels where the joyless transaction is completed in an exchange of money; human dump heaps like the Cité Nortier; desolate spots like l'Estrapade that give off the air of never having been inhabited at all; and, coursing through this, the great river, offering its oozy depths as a way one could end it all. The man sent here has no guides, no maps, no plans, no tools or weapons, no friends—except the streets, as he says. Jail and deportation are daily threats, and so is syphilis, of which he is reminded every time he visits a public toilet where the death's-head government posters warn that at his level of activity sex equals death. The fear of starvation stalks him, mocks him too as he reads the inviting restaurant menus posted in the windows. He does carry with him some fragile, flimsy hopes but finds gradually that hopes are not helps; they are instead only dangerous illusions, precisely because they blind him to the realities, sordid as they are, with which he must learn to live—or die. So, he must shed them, one by one, just as he sheds his tailor-made suits and every other bit of baggage that will hinder him as he plunges ever deeper into the wilderness. He consorts with the natives living close to the marrow of this place—whores, pimps, thieves like the Apaches who work the streets by night. He eats their food, even when it tastes like "the big toe of a cadaver," as he says of some rancid butter he is offered. The city, he finds, is "filled with poor people—the proudest and filthiest lot of beggars that ever walked the earth," and yet they have learned how to live here and to make a kind of gritty, hard triumph of their deprivation. Though he begins to take on their coloration because he finds it protective, his journey is not one of acquisition but instead one of spiritual debridement, the shedding of all those assumptions and unexamined beliefs he'd come here with, above all the hope that something, some event, some person or piece of luck—something *extrinsic*—will change his life. At last, shorn of everything, he finds himself "naked as a savage," at which point he becomes a renegade, one of those fearsome figures of frontier history who allegedly succumbed to the dark power of the wilderness and turned unnaturally against their own: the blood-drenched Simon Girty; John Tanner, captured by the Shawnee, then voluntarily living as an Ojibwa until at last he disappeared into the wilderness, a suspect in the murder of a white man. Or Kiowa Dutch. A German boy captured in Texas, Dutch grew into a huge, fierce warrior, riding with the Kiowa against the whites. He had forgotten his own language but had picked up a few obscene English expressions which he would hurl at the intruders in battle. But if Miller's narrator bears a telling resemblance to Kiowa Dutch, Miller would regard this as exemplary, a triumph of survival and not a surrender, for he has come through to a kind of clearing in what was at the outset only a featureless and bristling wilderness, where many of the weak go under. He, however, has learned through suffering and loss and isolation how to live without hope (which he sees as really illusion) but also without despair. He lives in the moment, in its brilliant specificity, asking nothing more of it than to see it clearly. "I don't give a fuck any more what's behind me," he says, "or what's ahead of me. I'm healthy. Incurably healthy. No sorrows, no regrets. No past, no future. The present is enough for me. Day by day. Today! *Le bel aujourd'hui* [The beautiful today]."

What is this if not the spiritual drama of the New World as it might have been? And what if such salvation were yet available? What if, after the plundering of the planet and the exploitation of its farthest reaches, its geographical and moral antipodes; after the extirpation of uncountable numbers of plants and animals and indigenous cultures: after all this, what if it should become clear at last that there will be no miracle that saves us from life itself? That there will be no mythy Isles of the Blessed, no terrestrial (or extra-terrestrial) paradise where ripe fruit never falls (to borrow from Wallace Stevens), no transcendental salvation? None of these. What if at last we should come somehow to the saving realization that there will only be *this*—whatever it is, roses and dung heap both—right here, right now? What if, like Miller's nameless picaro, we understood at the crater's rim that we are meant to live in this world as it is, to dig our hands into the mucky soil of its realities, to embrace it, to learn how to love it? This would not be the discovery of the hidden passage to the riches of Cathay but instead the inner discovery of that secret pass leading to true freedom, the freedom of the individual soul. At the same time, this would be an authentic escape—from the hopeless search for a way out of the inescapable conditions of human existence. And who knows? it might even ameliorate these just a bit.

After all its years as an outlaw book whose salacious passages were read to tatters by GIs and panting teenagers and tourists who wanted an imaginative stroll on the wild side, it might seem oxymoronic to speak of *Tropic of Cancer* as having a "moral." But when stripped of its rhetorical excesses, its comic boasts, its wild contradictions and coprolalia, it does have this spiritual arc. Maybe only an American, one exiled to the Old World against the tidal force of history, could have written it.

The story of Fillmore and his designing hooker that ends the book is microcosmic. And here, where it is to some extent at least possible to separate fact from fiction, the differences are instructive.

Richard Osborn did indeed like Fillmore suffer a mental breakdown, and for a time was institutionalized outside the city. He had been living with a younger French woman named Jeanne and somehow had become convinced he'd gotten her pregnant. At the same time as he keenly felt his obligation to Jeanne he was desperate to escape France for his own people in Bridgeport, Connecticut. Whether or not she was in fact pregnant, a professional, or merely an opportunist is questionable. But there is not much doubt that when Miller bumped into him outside a bank Osborn wanted nothing more out of life than to somehow escape the sorry mess he'd made of everything here in what for him was hardly "Gay Paree" any longer. For whatever reason—maybe merely for old times' sake— Miller decided to help him. He took the man in hand, went to the bank, the consulate, and then the station where he saw him aboard the boat train for Cherbourg and London. When he had done that he mailed Jeanne the money Osborn had provided for her—but not quite all of it, keeping about one hundred twenty-five dollars for himself.

What he made of this episode in *Tropic of Cancer* is distinctly rougher and harder on all concerned, most especially on his narrator, who is here depicted as a remorseless thief. Ginnette (Jeanne) comes off as a heartless whore and Fillmore as a spineless sort, willing enough to let his American friend clean up after him. Yet here again, beneath the fiction's shock value there lies Miller's grand theme, for Fillmore in his dissolute behavior in Paris and his subsequent flight over the sea to the New World replicates the whole sorry saga of the West that had covered the known world with blood and tyranny, making existence a mortal trial for the masses—and then had sailed away to repeat the saga in a place that ought to have been an unrepeatable opportunity to begin anew. And all of this for the same old reason: the refusal (or is it the inability?) to look at life's realities and be equal to their challenges and their opportunities. As long as France was wine, women, and money in his pocket, Fillmore was happy there, the narrator thinks. "And then, when he had had his fling, when the tent top flew off and he had a good look at the sky, he saw it wasn't a circus but an arena, just like everywhere. And a damned grim one." And so, off again he had gone on the same hopeless flight from reality to disillusionment.

As for the narrator, sitting there at bankside in the setting sun with a wad of bills in his pocket, it suddenly occurs to him that he too could now follow Fillmore, if he wished. He too could flee his parlous existence here. He could go back to his wife, could hear once again the sound of his native tongue, walk amidst the familiar sights of his old world. And yet, as he thinks of that old world—its realities as he had at some cost come to know them—he feels instantaneously how barren for him the prospect of America actually is: the spectral skyscrapers and beneath them the streets "choked with ants." He had been an ant once himself. That had been no circus, either, but a damned grim arena.

Beyond the few days the stolen cash would carry him his prospects here are not particularly bright, except for this: he is free at last of illusions, and he has made a place for himself, *here*. Just here. He has before him the remains of this day, this singular, unrepeatable moment of *Le bel aujourd'hui*. Paris has never looked better.

Coda

The writing of *Tropic of Cancer* probably gave Henry Miller the most intense artistic satisfaction of his life because it vindicated him in his conviction of who he was. Jack Kahane's publication of it, however, was something of an anticlimax for him, and maybe at that moment Anaïs Nin cared more about the book than its author did. By this point Miller was already furiously at work on *Tropic of Capricorn*, which was to be the story of Henry and June and thus was the return of the original muse. The writing of it doubtless contributed to the growing distance between Miller and the new muse Nin had become. Nin, however, continued to supply Miller with occasional cash gifts, but by the time Kahane published *Capricorn* in 1939 the Henry-Anaïs romance was really over, though neither would quite admit this. As for June, she had obtained a Mexican divorce from Miller the year *Cancer* was published in Paris. Not that much is known about her life after Henry except that it was bleak, a descending spiral of disasters that included electroshock therapy in the course of which she suffered a fall that conclusively broke her health. Miller managed to send her small sums of money in the 1940s, and they had one brief meeting in the fall of 1961 that was apparently unhappy for both of them. At some point thereafter June left the New York area for Arizona where a brother was living. It is believed that she died there, though the date of her death and the place of her burial are unknown.

The war had made Miller an exile from his beloved France in 1940. Back in America, he led a nomadic, hand-to-mouth existence for the next four years that replicated the one he had endured before he understood in Paris what his mission truly was. With this major difference, however: he now knew that he was a writer, an artist, and that he would be remembered even if his finest works, the *Tropics* and *Black Spring*, should remain forever banned in America. This made his hardships bearable, indeed even honorable to him, as a martyr's are. He tried writing pornography (Nin was doing the same). He set up as an astrologer. He turned out primitivistic watercolors in vast quantities and sold them for what he could get. He sent out what he called "begging letters" to friends, acquaintances, and institutions. He appears to have regarded these as a kind of literary genre. In 1942 he moved to the Los Angeles area and tried screenwriting. Two years later he moved to the isolated area of Big Sur, where he lived for the next nine years, in the course of which time fame found Henry Miller at last with the American publication of *Cancer.* It was an instant bestseller, as was *Capricorn* (1962). Now virtually anything of his, whether new, old, or recycled, found an enthusiastic audience, and he belatedly became a wealthy man. He also found himself enshrined as the somewhat aged satyr-king of unbridled sexuality. To an extent he had already been trading on this image for several years in his relationships with a succession of younger women, three of whom he married. The image gained validity in an ironic way when Nin published the portion of her diaries dealing with their affair: ironic because years before she had made him promise he would never draw on their relationship for literary capital. He never had. Yet now that he was a celebrity, Nin saw that she might capitalize on it and did.

In part to escape his fans and his fame, to which he had come to feel a profound ambivalence, Miller moved down to Pacific Palisades in 1963. He brought with him his entourage, his gofers, gatekeepers, and caregivers. But there was an anonymity there that he deeply craved now in these last days. A man, he said frequently, deserved to be let alone when he'd said everything he had to say, and Miller had. He died in his sleep on June 7, 1980.

Notes

1. In his poem "Voyage West," Archibald MacLeish has an outmoded, disgraced Columbus lamenting that "once the maps have all been made / A man were better dead than find new continents."

2. The truth of the horrific passage describing this episode has been questioned (but then, so for a couple of centuries were the rumors of Jefferson's relationship with his slave Sally Hemmings). When Crèvecoeur wrote, the literary tradition of travelers' tales was long established in Europe, the Near East, and the Orient. Crèvecoeur was occasionally in error about one thing and another, perhaps especially about the realities of Native American life, but these are *errors*, not a traveler's inventions, and the distinction is crucial. The tone of the passage is entirely consistent with the rest of his book, and I find little reason to believe he invented the encounter.

3. It is entirely possible that Crèvecoeur knew of a particularly shocking instance of frontier lawlessness, since it occurred in Pennsylvania and had been described by his friend Benjamin Franklin. This was the massacre of some peaceful Conestoga Indians in December 1763. At dawn on December 14, Irish

immigrant militiamen attacked a settlement of peaceful Conestogas near Lancaster, killing all six they found there and burning down the buildings. The Paxton Boys—as they came to be called—had wanted the Indians' land, land given them by William Penn as part of his "Holy Experiment." But there remained fourteen Conestogas left who might still make some claim on the land the Paxton Boys coveted. Therefore, on December 27, the Paxton Boys rode again, this time against the workhouse at Lancaster where the Conestoga refugees were housed. This time they finished the job and then settled on the conquered land. No charges were ever brought, and the Paxton Boys then decided to march on Philadelphia but were persuaded to turn back by a committee headed by Franklin.

4. In *Israel Potter* Herman Melville wrote thus of the Protean Ben Franklin: "Printer, postmaster, almanac maker, essayist, chemist, orator, tinker, statesman, humorist, philosopher, parlor man, political economist, professor of housewifery, ambassador, projector, maxim-monger, herb-doctor, wit:—Jack of all trades, master of each and mastered by none—the type and genius of his land."

5. Another Tennessee tall-talker once described for me what it was like hunting through a laurel thicket: "Son, it's like walking through a room full of rocking chairs at midnight."

6. One version of Quick's legend has it that when the Indians learned he had died they dug up his corpse, hacked it to pieces, and distributed these among their villages. Alas for them: Quick had died of smallpox, and so in death, he'd gotten his hundred and then some. Here is a specimen of the kind of humor the frontier experience contributed to the national culture.

7. Many years ago when I was on a magazine assignment in Barataria Bay a descendant of Nez Coupé Chighizola took me to the old pirate's crumbling grave. It was really empty now, he confided, because a hurricane had long ago "washed his carcass out to sea."

8. There is not much that links Miller to Robert Penn Warren, though they were roughly contemporaries. But surely Miller would have agreed with the autobiographical voice of Warren's poem "American Portrait: Old Style," where he remarks: "and

in that last summer / I was almost ready to learn / What the imagination is—it is only / The lie we must learn to live by, if ever / We mean to live at all."

9. In his brilliant introductory essay to Grove Press's first American edition of *Tropic of Cancer*, Karl Shapiro says Miller remained German to the end. "I have often thought," Shapiro continues, "that Germans make the best Americans, though they certainly make the worst Germans."

10. To be sure, we can never know precisely the tone and content of the talk of those Brooklyn boys of circa 1900. However, my own experiences of a south Chicago boyhood during World War II and afterward tell me that one of the ways a boy fit in with a neighborhood gang was to learn to use foul language and to sprinkle it liberally over his conversation. Surely the South Side can't have been unique in this. Not two years ago in my adopted hometown of Santa Fe I jokingly greeted an old friend at the service station one morning. "Go fuck yourself, Pat," I said as he came through the station door. "Did you hear that?" Pat asked the owner, Mike, without breaking stride. "I heard it," Mike replied. "That's nothing. When I was a kid in Astoria [Queens], you didn't say, 'Good morning, Pat,' 'Good morning, Fred,' when you saw one of your buddies on your way to the bus. You gave him the finger—way up high like this. And you hollered at him, '*Fuck you!*' If he didn't do that back to you, you knew something was wrong and that sooner or later you were gonna have to straighten it out with him."

11. The ethnic slurs used throughout the Clint Eastwood film *Gran Torino* (2009), while they are doubtless exaggerated for comic as well as thematic effect, are certainly not an unrealistic portrayal of this aspect of our culture.

12. The use of the word "outlaw" and his self-characterization as an "enemy of society" clearly belong to a chronologically later time than the reminiscence as a whole, one when Miller had lived long enough and achieved enough to begin regarding himself as a character, even as a work of art. In 1913 in the orchards of California this singular talent wouldn't have seemed a problem to him; it would instead have been protective, providing "Yorkie" with a cachet, tender hands, indifferent work habits, and all.

13. One is reminded here of Miller's artistic predecessor, Twain, who as a boy spied through the keyhole on the postmortem of the dead king, his father, and then much later wrote up a blazing, unsparing account of it. That account hasn't survived because William Dean Howells, who read it, urged that it be burned. The point here is that Twain's artistic impulse was to write what he'd seen, but subsequently he was persuaded to destroy it. Miller's description of his father asleep and snoring with his mummified face and blubbering lips is also unsparing, but he kept it and published it.

14. For a very long time now artists in various media have been trying to find a way back to some imagined Adamic state of spontaneity where no shadow falls between inspiration and execution. In painting, the discovery in the 1940s of decorated Paleolithic caves in France and Spain seemed to authenticate a period in human history where art truly was spontaneous, and the horses and aurochs simply flowed out of the artists' hands onto the rocky canvases. As we now know, these brilliant representations did not "flow." In Chinese and Japanese calligraphy where the artist's hand appears to be working much too rapidly to be guided by conscious thought, it is in fact being guided by a painstakingly acquired knowledge of *the way it is done*—by tradition, in other words. So, too, technologically sophisticated analysis of the Peche Merle cave in the Dordogne leads to the conclusion that the artists knew how the horses and mammoths ought to look before committing the first stroke. The process is convincingly illustrated in Jeanne-Pierre Baux's documentary film *Prehistoric Art in the Quercy Region* (Vanves, France, 1999).

15. Many months thereafter, when Miller held a part-time job at the paper, Root met him but never knew him well.

16. In a *New York Review of Books* essay on the Royal Academy of Arts exhibition of Van Gogh's letters and accompanying illustrations, Richard Dorment makes the salient point for us about Miller's artistic situation in Paris at the beginning of the '30s. "Though the act of creation is highly personal," he writes, "it rarely happens in isolation. . . . The unrecognized genius who dies alone in his garret is largely a myth." The Van Gogh revealed in letters, sketches, and paintings was no solitary mad-

man, Dorment says, but instead a thoughtful artist well aware of art history and what his contemporaries were doing. Many years before, Miller had come to the same conclusion about Van Gogh in *The Books in My Life* (1952). As for Miller himself, he was far too gregarious to have remained alone in Paris. He made friends, and by the time he left at the outset of World War II he had quite a few of them. But he had very few friends who were writers, none who were trying to do what he was. His path toward *Tropic of Cancer* was in many significant ways his own, which accounts in part for the singularity of the book's voice, vision, and imagery. The Parisian avant-garde opened his eyes, but what he saw was singular.

17. Over the nine years he spent in France, Miller gradually acquired a substantial knowledge of French history and culture and learned to speak and write the language passably. But his understanding of France never remotely approached his astonishing grasp of his native culture.

18. Customarily, he spent it on cigarettes, coffee, wine, postage, and the *métro*.

19. Years later, he remembered his audience to have been the American painter John Nichols, one of the regulars at the Auguste Bartholdi flat, who was working on a portrait of Miller that depicted him as a savage being.

20. In recent years a spirited debate has been joined about exactly what constitutes the purely documentary in still photography and cinematography, some of it centering on the work of two of America's finest documentarians, Walker Evans and Dorothea Lange. The great Robert Doisneau sometimes posed his human subjects in his documentary photographs of Paris, something Brassaï appears not to have done in his nighttime shots of the city's life.

21. Le Zeyer is still there and still dishing out *choucroute* and seafood.

22. One version of Miller at Villa Seurat in the summer of '31 has him typing on the versos of the manuscript of *Crazy Cock*. If a story is really good, someone cynically said, it probably isn't true. Still . . .

23. Like a good many other episodes in Miller's life, much of the

June-Henry-Anaïs ménage, which begins here, remains murky, probably permanently so. The ménage has, of course, generated a good deal more heat than light and inevitably more of both of these than on its effect on *Tropic of Cancer*. We don't know just when June arrived, for starters. If she was already in Paris when Nin invited Miller to dinner, how was that arranged? We don't know how or why June showed up for the second dinner invitation or what Nin's motivation may have been for beginning a dalliance with her and whether it ever became physical. We don't know what Miller's attitude toward the women's relationship was, whether it was to him an awful reminder of the June-Jean affair; or whether he was in some sense attracted to its possibilities for him, sexually and artistically, or both at once. My treatment of it here tries—perhaps not completely successfully—to concentrate on its implications for the composition of *Tropic of Cancer*.

24. Surviving photographs of June do not capture the remarkable impression she made on those meeting her for the first time. Miller's rapturous recollection has been mentioned earlier and might be discounted for obvious reasons. But there is this one from Nin and Brassaï's as well. When Miller introduced them, Brassaï recalled that what struck him was a "neck as long as a swan's emerging from a tight black velour dress, a neck out of a Modigliani painting." Baudelaire, he went on, "who loved the art and artifice of a woman's face, would have swooned at the feet of this creature."

25. He never did. *Tropic of Capricorn* bears closest comparison, but it is a more polished piece of literature, whereas *Cancer*, for all its revisions, retains the raw quality of a vivisection.

26. Miller himself wasn't thrilled by Rosset's hard-won victory (the result of more than sixty separate legal proceedings). He had never been keen on having *Cancer* published in America, precisely because its continued status as an outlawed book confirmed his own status as a renegade, as well as his view of America as a brainless, bloated, anti-life monster, hell-bent on warping the rest of the world into its own image. Rosset's win, he felt, had the effect of making him seem a part of the grand march of Amer-

ican freedom and of transmogrifying his public image from renegade to celebrity.

27. "Literature is news that STAYS news," said Ezra Pound, who
     immediately appreciated Miller's achievement in *Cancer.*

28. Miller is in distinguished company here. The first of the Four
     Noble Truths taught by the Buddha is commonly translated as
     "suffering," but more loosely and more accurately as a dissatis-
     faction with the inevitable conditions of our existence. In Bud-
     dhist thought this is regarded as the gateway to the Dharma.
     Similarly, Freud regarded life's inevitable demands as "too hard
     for us." We are always in need, therefore, he argued in *Civiliza-
     tion and Its Discontents,* of various "palliative remedies." These
     range from religion to intoxicating substances—*anything* that
     numbs us to the otherwise unbearable.

Selected Bibliography

Allen, Robert G. *Horrible Prettiness: Burlesque and American Culture.* Chapel Hill: University of North Carolina Press, 1991.

Asbury, Herbert. *The French Quarter: An Informal History of the New Orleans Underworld.* New York: Ballantine, 1974.

———. *The Gangs of New York: An Informal History of the Underworld.* New York: Thunder's Mouth, 1998.

Bakeless, John. *The Eyes of Discovery: The Pageant of North America as Seen by the First Explorers.* New York: Dover, 1961.

Bernier, Olivier. *Fireworks at Dusk: Paris in the Thirties.* Boston: Little, Brown, 1993.

Blair, Walter. *Native American Humor, 1800–1900.* New York: American Book Company, 1937.

Brassaï. *Henry Miller: The Paris Years.* Translated by Timothy Bent. New York: Arcade, 1995.

———. *The Secret Paris of the '30s.* Translated by Richard Miller. New York: Pantheon, 1976.

Coates, Robert M. *The Outlaw Years: The History of the Land Pirates of the Natchez Trace.* New York: Literary Guild of America, 1930.

Crèvecoeur, J. Hector St. John de. *Letters from an American Farmer.* Bedford, Massachusetts: Applewood, n.d.

Dearborn, Mary V. *The Happiest Man Alive: A Biography of Henry Miller.* New York: Simon & Schuster, 1991.

Dorment, Richard. "The Passions of Vincent van Gogh." *New York Review of Books* 57, no. 5 (March 25, 2010): 16–18.

Ferguson, Robert. *Henry Miller: A Life.* New York: W. W. Norton, 1991.

Freud, Sigmund. *Civilization and Its Discontents.* Translated by Joan Riviere. Garden City, New York: Doubleday Anchor, 1958.

De Haan, Panda, and Ludo Van Halem. "Miró in Holland: The Dutch Interiors, 1928." *Rijksmuseum Bulletin* 38 (2010): 211–245.

Hamsun, Knut. *Hunger.* Translated by Robert Bly. New York: Farrar, Straus and Giroux, 2008.

Hutchinson, E. R. *Tropic of Cancer on Trial: A Case History of Censorship.* New York: Grove, 1969.

Kenny, Kevin. *Peaceable Kingdom Lost: The Paxton Boys and the Destruction of William Penn's Holy Experiment.* New York: Oxford University Press, 2004.

Kessel, Joseph. *Belle de Jour.* Translated by Geoffrey Wagner. New York: Overlook Duckworth, 2007.

Lawrence, D. H. *Studies in Classic American Literature.* New York: Penguin, 1977.

Mailer, Norman. *Genius and Lust: A Journey Through the Major Writings of Henry Miller.* New York: Grove, 1976.

Martin, Jay. *Always Merry and Bright: The Life of Henry Miller.* Santa Barbara: Capra; London: Sheldon, 1979.

Matthiessen, Peter. *Wildlife in America.* New York: Viking, 1975.

Melly, George. *Paris and the Surrealists.* New York: Thames and Hudson, 1991.

Miller, Henry. *The Air-Conditioned Nightmare.* New York: New
Directions, 1970.

———. *Black Spring.* New York: Grove, 1989.

———. *The Books in My Life.* New York: New Directions, n.d.

———. *Crazy Cock.* New York: Grove Weidenfeld, 1991.

———. *Letters to Emil.* Edited by George Wickens. New York:
New Directions, 1989.

———. *Moloch, or, This Gentile World.* New York: Grove, 1992.

———. *My Life and Times.* New York: Gemini Smith, n.d.

———. *Remember to Remember.* New York: New Directions,
1947.

———. *The Time of the Assassins: A Study of Rimbaud.* New
York: New Directions, 1962.

———. *Tropic of Cancer.* Shelton, Connecticut: First Edition
Library, n.d.

———. *Tropic of Capricorn.* New York: Grove, 1965.

Nin, Anaïs. *The Diary of Anaïs Nin.* Volume one, 1931–1934.
Edited by Gunther Stuhlmann. San Diego: Harcourt, 1994.

———. *Henry and June.* From *A Journal of Love: The Unexpur-
gated Diary of Anaïs Nin, 1931–1932.* Orlando: Harcourt,
1993.

O'Gorman, Edmundo. *The Invention of America: An Inquiry
into the Historical Nature of the New World and the Meaning of
Its History.* Bloomington: Indiana University Press, 1961.

Porter, Bern, ed. *The Happy Rock: A Book About Henry Miller.*
Berkeley: Packard, 1945.

Ray, Man. *Self-Portrait.* Boston: Bullfinch Press, Little, Brown,
1999.

Reynolds, Michael. *Hemingway in the 1930s.* New York: W. W.
Norton, 1997.

Richardson, Robert D. *First We Read, Then We Write: Emerson
on the Creative Process.* Iowa City: University of Iowa Press,
2009.

Roche, Charlotte. *Wetlands.* Translated by Tim Mohr. New
York: Grove, 2009.

Root, Waverly. *The Paris Edition: The Autobiography of Waverly Root, 1927–1934*. San Francisco: North Point, 1987.

Rourke, Constance. *American Humor: A Study of the National Culture*. New York: New York Review, 2004.

Sayag, Alain, and Annick Lionel-Marie, eds. *Brassaï, The Monograph*. Boston: Bullfinch Press, Little, Brown, 2000.

Shattuck, Roger. *The Banquet Years: The Origins of the Avant-Garde in France, 1885 to World War I*. New York: Vintage, 1968.

Smith-Rosenberg, Carroll. *This Violent Empire: The Birth of an American National Identity*. Chapel Hill: University of North Carolina Press, 2010.

Snyder, Robert. *This Is Henry, Henry Miller from Brooklyn: Conversations with the Author from "The Henry Miller Odyssey."* Los Angeles: Nash, 1974.

Tanner, John. *A Narrative of the Captivity and Adventures of John Tanner During Thirty Years Residence Among the Indians of the Interior of North America*. Harmondsworth, United Kingdom: Penguin, 1994.

Turner, Frederick. *Beyond Geography: The Western Spirit Against the Wilderness*. New York: Viking, 1980.

——, ed. *The Portable North American Indian Reader*. New York: Viking, 1974.

Vidal, Gore. *Inventing a Nation: Washington, Adams, Jefferson*. New Haven: Yale University Press, 2003.

Whitman, Walt. *Leaves of Grass: The First (1855) Edition*. New York: Viking, 1973.

Acknowledgments

I am indebted to the following friends for advice, encouragement, technical assistance, and the gift or loan of relevant books: Glenn Bokhof, Kay Carlson, Eudice Daly, Les Daly, Kai Erikson, Fitch Himmelright, Joyce Idema, Phillip King, Dierdre Ling, Dana Newmann, Eugene Newmann, Nicholas Potter, Steve Reed, Ileene Smith, Robin Straus, Aaron Turner.

Index

Note: The abbreviation HM in subheadings refers to Henry Miller